MW00618552

It's More Than Fishing

Larry McKinney, General Editor
John W. Tunnell Jr., Founding Editor

With the support of Kathie and Ed Cox Jr. Books on Conservation Leadership through the Texas Natural Resource Conservation Publication Endowment, Meadows Center for Water and the Environment, Texas State University

Thanks to Pat for making a difference in the Gulf of Mexico and in Texas
—Will and Pam Harte

It's More

The Art of Texas

Than Fishing

Trout and Redfish Angling

Pat Murray

TEXAS A&M UNIVERSITY PRESS
COLLEGE STATION

Copyright © 2020 by Patrick D. Murray
All rights reserved
First edition

This paper meets the requirements of ANSI/NISO Z39.48–1992
(Permanence of Paper).
Binding materials have been chosen for durability.
Manufactured in China through Four Colour Print Group.

Library of Congress Cataloging-in-Publication Data

Names: Murray, Patrick D., author.
Title: It's more than fishing: the art of Texas trout and redfish angling
  / Patrick D. Murray.
Other titles: Harte Research Institute for Gulf of Mexico Studies series;
  no. 35.
Description: First edition. | College Station: Texas A&M University Press,
  [2020] | Series: Harte Research Institute for Gulf of Mexico Studies
  series; number thirty-five | Includes index.
Identifiers: LCCN 2019057881 | ISBN 9781623498153 | ISBN 9781623498160
  (ebook)
Subjects: LCSH: Fishing—Texas—Gulf Coast. | Brook trout
  fishing—Texas—Gulf Coast. | Red drum fishing—Texas—Gulf Coast. |
  Fishes—Conservation—Texas—Gulf Coast.
Classification: LCC SH551 .M87 2020 | DDC 799.17/554—dc23
LC record available at https://lccn.loc.gov/2019057881

A list of titles in this series is available at the end of the book.

Contents

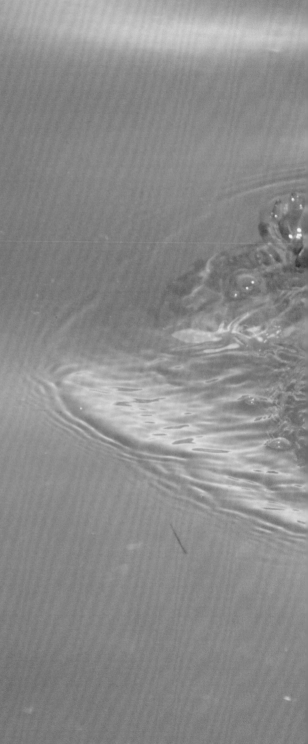

1

Overview

WHEN I WROTE my first book on fishing, *Pat Murray's No-Nonsense Guide to Coastal Fishing*, in 2001 through Texas Fish & Game Publishing, I could not imagine I would ever write another book on fishing for speckled trout and redfish in Texas. I really did not feel like I had anything else relevant to say. Then, after almost two decades and seemingly countless additional fishing experiences, it struck me that I wanted to write a new book from a different perspective while still digging into some of the key skills for successful angling, the insights of some of the amazing anglers I know and have known, the brilliance of the cast of world-class scientists I get to work with, and perspectives that come from a lot of hours working in the marine conservation space rather than just my own reflections (although here you will still note an abundance of personal reflections). I also wanted to leverage, retouch, update, and in some cases even reprint some positively received content and articles that I have written for various magazines (mainly the Coastal Conservation Association's [CCA's] *Tide* magazine) through this past decade and try to address a few nontraditional approaches to our beloved art of fishing.

I wrote my no-nonsense guide shortly after concluding a personally rewarding run of professional fish guiding in the Galveston Bay area

and while I was still actively participating in saltwater fishing tournaments. I had a lot of opinions and probably a lot more certainty about a number of aspects of Texas coastal fishing. By contrast, I write this book from a completely different personal perspective after years of working in marine resource conservation, fishing a much broader diversity of locations and styles, and frequently fishing under the guidance of others' expertise. Undoubtedly, it is a very different perspective, and maybe that very fact speaks best to the notion that the art of fishing is constantly evolving both among our collective angling public and with all of us individually.

It is ironic that the longer I pursue angling, be it speckled trout and redfish on the Texas coast or chinook salmon in the Pacific Northwest, I find out how much there still is to learn about this dynamic art. I have definitely come to find that the two best sources for improvement are personal experience and the vast wisdom of others. Experience is critical and is the slow multiplier that we all must figure through to improve any and all skills. It takes practice and experience to reach the level of true excellence. Although daunting, it really makes sense. From classical musicians to master sushi chefs to everyday anglers, experience builds the priceless knowledge that is often mislabeled as instinct.

Additionally, the wisdom of others is the potion that can cause leaps and sprinting dashes of advancement. One bit of advice or unique perspective can forever change the way you pursue your passion. I can recall several moments through the years when true experts like the late David Wright or tenacious active guides like James Plaag would casually mention the underpinnings of a fishing trend and a light would turn on. Many of those lights still guide my fishing today.

The internet has forever changed the dissemination of expertise. Gone are the days of secret spots and secret patterns. The real key now is to avoid information overload. Expose yourself to as much information from reliable sources as you can, but always remember to distill it down to the insights and strategies that matter. Don't chase the next best spot, bait, pattern, or idea—it will most likely not lead you to fish but rather to another sketchy scheme or plan to catch fish next time or the next time or the next time. . . . I think we all have experienced that at some point.

Clearly, fishing is much more of an art than science. As anglers, we are constantly trying to discern "patterns" and other definitive truths for success that unfortunately often change as regularly as tides. A reef that was a "no miss" last year is mysteriously dead this year. The shoreline that always produced big trout in spring is now covered with redfish but has no indication of a trout. Everything changes—the patterns of fish, the movement of baitfish, the structure of the bay, and the very flow of the tides through the bay and marsh. It all changes. The only constant in fishing is that the fish are still trying to avoid being caught as much today as they did one hundred or a thousand years ago. To improve as anglers, we must be willing to change and evolve—learn patterns and also learn to ignore them. I know that sounds annoyingly transcendental, but it is true. It has been an eye-opening experience for me to reread this book after writing it and find a number of almost contradictory statements I wrote through various chapters. Most are subtle or caveated but nonetheless are present. I think that speaks to the very nature of fishing. If you are static and unwavering, you are probably also not catching fish. Be comfortable with contradiction.

I am reminded every day that one should never assume or even entertain the idea that you might be the most experienced, smartest, best equipped, or for that matter even correct about many aspects of fishing. Writing this book has reminded me of that repeatedly. The collective knowledge and experience of the experts and novices I have known, fished with, watched, and interviewed for this book would take volumes to completely unpack . . . and those are just the ones I know. I have only scraped the surface. Clearly, there is an ocean of experience and expertise out there. Although I believe this book is a reasonable yield of fishing insight, I hope it helps you embark on a far broader and never-ending search for more information.

In building *It's More Than Fishing*, I expanded and revisited a few features that I have previously addressed in recent years, including a look at the basics of patterning, my adoration of the Texas surf, the timeless insights of marine biologist anglers, and the value of guide selection. As an aside, I write so much about hiring a guide because it is so incredibly valuable for developing your skills. I added several new characters in my ongoing saga of torturing experts by forcing them to isolate their lure selection to five baits in the "If I Could Only Pick Five" chapter. It explores the picks an angler might make if you could only fish with five baits for the rest of time. It's hard to adequately describe how painful it is for these experts to pare their picks down to five, but their writhing yields a lot of insight and some true entertainment. Through the years, every time I explore this topic, I get an abundance of feedback from interested anglers. I dug into innovation, discovering patterns and a few other topics I adore, and I simply had to address modern marine resource conservation. I have spent more than two decades pursuing marine conservation as a profession, so I had to share some contemporary thoughts regarding it and the critically important role recreational anglers play in it. I also added a couple of chapters that address tips and tactics that have improved my art. Finally, you will notice a list of key points at the start of most chapters. I have really grown to like the summaries that appear at the start of many of the columns, textbooks, and online articles I read and thought a similar convention might be of use in this book.

As you read, remember that fishing is fishing. Nothing will ever change that. Like so many things in our shared society, technology and the internet portend to make things easier, but many of these sources only make things more complicated and simply track our often-wandering journey at a faster pace. Focus on the joy of pursuing the art of fishing, and your passion will never die and, most importantly, your skill will never stop improving. I know I work at it every time I go.

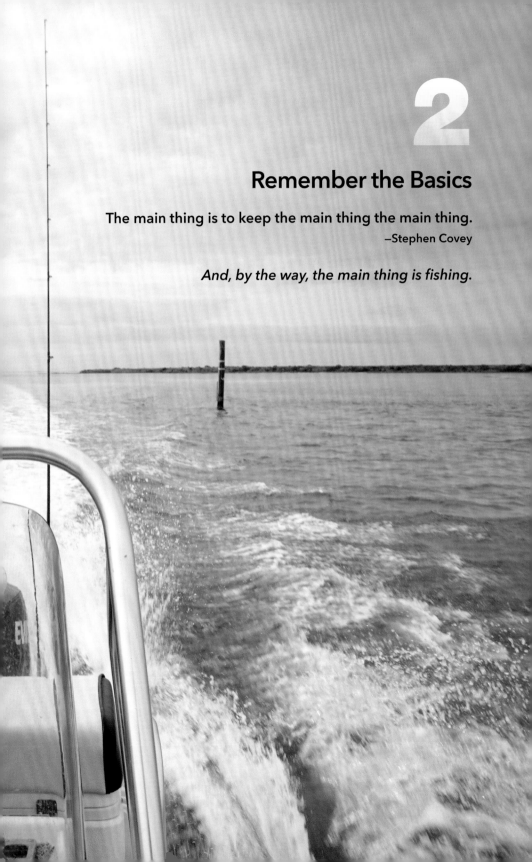

2

Remember the Basics

The main thing is to keep the main thing the main thing.
—Stephen Covey

And, by the way, the main thing is fishing.

KEY POINTS

- The funny thing about the "basics" is that they never change. They are as true today as they were before recreational angling even existed. They are the fundamentals of tracking any animal, and in this case, our target lives in an utterly different realm than us, is cold-blooded, and really does not want to be caught.

- Look for baitfish. Although never a guarantee, the presence of baitfish activity is one of the most consistent fish signs.

- Confidence is key. It is earned through hard work, experience, and observing excellence.

- Fish signs matter. Remember that identifying them is important, but you have to put in the work of fishing them thoroughly to unlock the pattern.

- Learn the layout of the bay to understand its flow. Start with a map to provide a virtual flyover to get you in sync with the flow of the bay.

- Never stop exploring. There may not be a lot of new spots left on the Texas coast, but there are always new and emerging patterns to explore.

THE BASICS are still the basics, yet many anglers ignore them. I guess that is true for most art forms, but fishing seems rife with an attention deficit disorder–like approach to the cornerstones of finding fish and actually getting them to bite.

The funny thing about the "basics" is that they never change. They are as true today as they were before recreational angling even existed. They are the fundamentals of tracking any animal, and in this case, our target lives in an utterly different realm than us, is cold-blooded, and really does not want to be caught.

I have had the luxury of being around and fishing with some amazingly gifted anglers and true fish trackers who can make success look easy, and the one commonality with all of them is their inseparable appreciation for and utilization of some of the most basics elements of fishing. They have the core tenets of angling burned into their thinking, to the point that they do not have to consciously focus. Not unlike a great basketball player at the free throw line or a legendary batter at the plate, they instinctively make the moves that put them in the best possible position for success. With the basics instilled, everything is done with ease. And, among those who I truly respect, I have yet to find one who is born with that. They all earn it by working hard and passionately at their art and making sure that sound basics are at the heart of every decision. In his book *Outliers*, author Malcolm Gladwell cites the now famous ten thousand–hour principle as the basis of all exceptional people and performances. He follows the paths of a number of outliers (think Bill Gates or the Beatles) and how the extraordinary amount of time they put into their passion made them exceptional. If you think about it, that speaks to the same tenet of mastering the basics. The only way to truly master the key elements of your passionate pursuit is by putting in the hours.

Additionally, focus is a critical part in avoiding the lure of distraction and making sure the basics are the foundation of your fishing decisions. Warren Buffett famously cites his appreciation for being in Omaha as opposed to New York City as a component of his investing focus. He makes the astute point that there are a flood of assumedly great ideas in New York every day, and he only needs a few really good ones every year. This biting insight strikes to the very point of the importance of focusing on the basics. There are a thousand new techniques, baits, retrieves, types of gear, and spots for any given day or even minute of fishing, but the fundamental truths of tracking fish are at the roots of 99 percent of all good fishing decisions. Make sure you know the fundamentals and then ensure that you actually focus and follow them.

Look for Bait

As anyone who has vacantly waded through rafts of mullet or clouds of menhaden knows, angling success is not always as easy as locating bait. There are plenty of times that gamefish are not with the bait or, worse, they are . . . and you simply do not know it. There is not a 100 percent correlation between locating bait and locating fish, but it is pretty close. Find bait and a lot of times you have found the school of fish you are seeking.

The cooler the water temperature, the more important this becomes. Summer is likely the most difficult season in that the bays, flats, and

beachfront often load up with every imaginable size and type of bait-fish, but the chilling temperatures of fall and winter can make even an occasional mullet flip a neon-quality sign.

The funny thing is that locating bait is sometimes only half the battle. You also have to actually stick with the area that has bait and fish it with focus. I vividly remember a stagnant summer morning on Galveston's east beach when the bait was stacked tight to the almost nonexistent beach break in water just below the knee. I quickly dismissed the clicking shad and occasional vaulting mullet as I earnestly chugged out to the second bar. The water was a perfect hazy green and completely devoid of any life. I diligently ground away and (of course) caught nothing. Any number of times I would glance back at the beach line, dismissing it as idle bait in super shallow water. My bite was sure to turn on . . . but it didn't. In a final move of desperation before heading back to my truck, I eased up to the bank and flipped a pumpkinseed Bass Assassin rigged on a $\frac{1}{16}$-oz. jighead into the bait. . . . you can guess the rest. It was a mosaic of every beachfront species and enough quality trout to make my morning exceptional.

What struck me the most in this experience was my unwavering ability to dismiss a fundamental fish sign because I had imposed the idea that the water was way too shallow, and I had not caught fish consistently in the often-shallow edge of the Galveston surf. Even in the face of no signs of life, I immediately went to my comfort depth on the second bar and mindlessly fished empty water. It was a booming reminder not only to honor the presence of baitfish, but also to always follow the best available fish signs, even if they do not fit my perception of being viable.

Confidence

Confidence matters. This is true in all pursuits, and angling is no different. If you do not have confidence, you simply are not going to find fish with any consistency. That is an incredibly common malady. We have all known the guy or gal who has the correct equipment, plenty of experience, a decent knowledge of the bay, and still can't catch fish. I've known that guy, seen that guy, and occasionally am that guy. It's like a virus that lurks in all of us. You can absolutely control it and force it into remission, but all it takes is a couple of missed surefire strategies coupled with humbling cleaning-table experiences to let that confidence-crashing virus loose in your system again.

This problem actually deserves some form of diagnostic terminology, like "Confidence Dysfunction." Maybe some enterprising pharmaceutical company will create a pill to cure CD, but until then, the key is to not overthink it. That angler who does will never be consistent or likely even very good at pursuing his passion. The strugglers tend to talk a lot about the love of the sunrise and how "it's just great being out on the water," but they really don't mean that. What they are screaming is that they wish they were hooked up during that beautiful sunrise out on the water and that struggling is a downer. We've all been there, and ultimately, it is the difficult reclamation of confidence that will bring us back out of that slump.

Remember that confidence cannot be bought, stolen, or even borrowed. You have to earn it. It often comes from the previously mentioned ten thousand hours of hard labor and a humble approach to learning from and observing others. As you build your skills and acknowledge your advances, the confidence will always follow.

Gearing Up

Like many passion-driven pursuits, we spend a lot of time and money focusing way too much on the gear and not nearly enough on the skills. There is a great quote that I reference throughout this book: "It is always about the archer and never about the arrows." This perfectly captures the odd habit of most anglers to gear themselves to the point of distraction and not focus on the basic tools for fishing.

Think about some of greatest artists, photographers, chefs, and musicians that had and even still have gear that would be considered rudimentary at best. Ask most great chefs what kitchen tools you really need, and they will produce a strikingly short list. We anglers should always remember that.

Gear is fun and important, but no amount of gear nor any given piece of it is going to make you the angler you truly want to be. As you outfit your boat, wading belt, tackle box, or whatever stores your gear, allow need to drive your selections over want. This is the underlying point of the "If I Could Only Pick Five" chapter of this book. By focusing on what you really need to help you make your trip, you will free yourself up from the illusion that gear makes the angler.

Author's note: My selection for Texas trout and redfish fishing is simple and easy. I like 6' 6" G. Loomis GLX and IMX rods and small Shimano baitcast reels (I currently use outdated Chronarch 50s, but the new models are tremendous as well). I have used that general rod and reel combination for many, many years and not seen anything to make me change yet. I use monofilament line (I still think braid might be witchcraft) and tie direct to my lures with a basic fisherman's knot. I have a wading belt with a set of pliers, stringer holder, and pouch for my lure box. You really do not need anything else. I am a fan of Simms wading boots and basic waders (during winter) and am a huge believer in AFTCO's Samurai hoodie shirt and Original fishing pants for sun protection and super light fabric. Combine that with a pair of Costa sunglasses and basic selection of lures to address all levels of the water column, and I am ready for any flat, bay reef, shoreline, or beachfront.

Fish Signs

They matter. As a matter of fact, they really matter.

I opened this chapter with a brief exploration of the key sign of bait-fish, but in this section, I want to highlight the broad picture of fish signs, the atypical ways they appear, and their vital role in success.

Fish signs are our only real-time clues to the fin prints of the fish we are tracking. We can go to historically productive spots based on memories of past trips, but to consistently succeed, it takes an attention to (and a certain amount of expertise reading of) fish signs. Countless articles, books, and blog posts have explored every type of sign, from slicks to mud boils, and that is definitely worth reviewing, but honestly, in the past decade, the basic mystery of what a fish sign is has largely evaporated from the modern bay angler's mind. Most know that a slick appears as an oily patch on the surface and has a somewhat sweet almost watermelon or cutgrass smell, or that birds hovering low to the water is often a sign of baitfish being herded to the surface. There is nothing innovative about any of these insights, which have been in writing for many decades. The real trick to applying any of the classic fish signs is to pay attention to your surroundings and be willing to try them out.

One of the most vivid examples I can remember of this was many years ago along the Houston Ship Channel. On the lower end of the channel, a significant amount of spoil had been dumped on the eastern side of the channel on an existing washed-out spoil area. It was not a big production, but within a short period, there were a series of high-relief mud humps that rose from the sludge of the channel edge to five or six feet of water. For the most part, among the group I guided with and fished around, none of us really saw it as noteworthy or even knew that the humps were there. One day while crossing the channel, an angler (my memory is that it was the extraordinary angler Maurice Estlinbaum) saw an abundance of slicks pouring out of a very nontraditional area. He set up a drift and quickly found some remarkably good trout fishing. Apparently, that newly deposited spoil had all of the ingredients to aggregate trout in what was previously nothing more than a featureless deep mud flat.

This unique find speaks to the point that tracking fish is truly a two-step process. You have to identify the tracks in whatever form you find them, and then be willing to actually commit the time and effort to figure out the pattern. Interestingly, these humps produced consistently but in diminishing returns until the natural current and wakes of the passing tankers and freighters shaved them back out of existence.

It is important to note that these transient humps are not an exclusive event. There are countless examples of new or emerging structures creating new patterns. Reefs grow, spoil moves, currents shift, but the basic tenets of tracking fish largely stay the same. The trick is to make sure you are not so busy going to where you think the fish are that you step right over an emerging or undiscovered path.

Learn the Flow of the Bay

The most common trap for limiting your understanding of any bay system (regardless of how long you have fished it) is to think of it as a collection of spots and not as the dynamic continuum that it is. Honestly, the longer someone fishes a bay, the easier it becomes to fall into this trap. You run from spot A to J and back to B and then wrap up your day. It's a dangerous habit. It is what keeps many anglers from truly mastering the bays they regularly fish and makes you incredibly less effective in the new ones you are exploring.

As silly as it sounds, one of the best tools for getting a true feel for a bay or bay system is to download a map and start viewing it from a distant perspective. Think of it as a flyover where you are looking for the broad contours, what rivers or marsh fuel it, how it sits in proximity to the ocean, and what impact the wind and current likely have on it. Gradually zoom in on the particulars of the bay and notice every curve and contour. Think about the fact that bay bottoms tend to soften toward river and bayou mouths and harden closer to ocean passes and areas of strong regular tide flow. Also, think about likely movements of bait species in various seasons. All of these observations matter.

When I apply this analysis to any bay, I am reminded of the world-class largemouth bass anglers who travel great distances to fish completely unfamiliar lakes and somehow put together tournament-winning bags of fish. They embody that spirit of learning and willingness to pull away from specific spots and storied techniques to earn a genuine understanding of the body of water they are currently fishing. I think we all can learn from that regardless of where we fish. Learn the bays you

frequent, but remember to take a step back occasionally and allow yourself to take a fresh, unfixed look and reevaluate. You may see something
you regularly overlook.

Explore

Not enough can be written or spoken about the need to explore. We
get so set in our patterns and forget that every spot was new once. It
sounds trite, but this is the most fundamental of all of the basics if you
really think about it. Without exploration, we would not even know
our coastal bays existed. We would have never discovered redfish
swimming in shallow waters or speckled trout wandering to a near-
shore platform. All of the Lost Lakes and Dead Man's Holes across our
coasts would still be true to their names . . . but they're not because of
explorers. Much of the big exploration is long gone. I can assure you
that Galveston Bay has been discovered, but it doesn't mean that there
are not countless untested and emerging patterns every day. There is
always something new to explore.

3

Lure Color Doesn't Matter ...
Until It Does

Go fish!

KEY POINTS

- Unfortunately, lure color can matter tremendously in certain situations. Make sure you bring baits that cover both dark and light shades. Think plum, dark red, and shades of black to cover the dark, and bring clear, light chartreuse, and gray shades for the light.

- Every color of topwater bait can have its day in the victory circle, but the classic colors of chrome and bone are always good bets.

- Be open to new designs, shades, and combinations for sure, but with limited space in any wading belt box and countless colors of tails, plugs, topwaters, and spoons available, stick to baits that you know consistently get results.

- Color selection will always matter, but confidence and skill always beat color.

I HATE WHEN lure color matters. Many, many times it is largely meaningless, but there are times when it matters. . . . sometimes a lot. We have all experienced it. You stand in your boat or on a shoreline or flat watching another angler who is dialed in on the fish. At first, you convince yourself that he is merely on an isolated school and you subconsciously (or maybe slightly consciously) ease toward him. Bracing for your turn, you confidently work away, waiting for the bite that never comes. You think, "Maybe I just need to slow it down a little." No luck, and you keep slowly oozing your increasingly sleazy self toward the guy who is still on fire. Eventually, you stoop to desperation and shout the question of shame. "Hey man, what cha throwing?" As the words leave your mouth, you realize that it actually sounds even more pathetic out loud than it did in your head. It's a horrible sinking moment brought on by the desperation of failed angling. I'm actually not even sure why any one of us would ask. Invariably, the angler is wrapped in imperious confidence and either will choose to ignore you or will yell back something meaningless like "a jig." It's a debasing moment that leads you to spend your entire next paycheck at the fishing tackle store to buy every lure that looks like the faintest images you had of Captain Fantastic's miracle lure. It's the reason that tackle stores have rows and rows of bait color choices. Think about it. If it really didn't matter as much as I wish it didn't, a fishing tackle shop would fit in a small apartment rather than sprawling out like a department store.

The main problem with lure color mattering is that it introduces the shadow of doubt into all of those times that you are not getting bites. "Maybe I should have tried the lemon-chicken-sunrise paddle tail, and I would have definitely caught fish." I get this dialectic rolling in my head that maybe if I had a different bait I would be getting bites, but if I constantly change baits, I am not focusing on actually patterning the fish, but maybe the fish won't bite this bait regardless of my efforts to pattern, so maybe I should change baits. . . . It's a brutal feedback loop.

I can live with the fact that certain bait styles can actually matter, but color is a lot harder to accept. If I choose to throw a topwater all day and never try a jig, that is my self-limiting choice. I know that a number of bait choices will regularly not produce even when you are on fish, and other baits will. That's OK, but if color choice is the problem? That's an angler's nightmare.

So, How Do You Combat It?

I think every angler has to acknowledge general patterns in color selection. Regardless of whether you are pulling plastic for blue marlin

150 miles offshore or suspending a ⅟₃₂-oz. jig for bluegill, there are general themes that are worth adhering to in your color selection.

Make sure you fill out both dark and light shades. That may appear overly simplistic, but I believe this helps break down color selection into broad categories. When you think dark, target the dark reds, plums, and the important shades and versions of black. These choices tend to provide little-to-no transparency and logically have a full silhouette for both jigs and plugs. It is not coincidental that dark colors can be particularly effective in off-color water and at night. I presume the deeper shade presents the broadest presence.

To me, the light category can be as literal as a clear glow, subtlety shaded chartreuse, or natural light brown and gray. These parts of the color spectrum are logically going to present a subtle shade. My confidence is highest with these colors in relatively to extremely clear water. I am particularly fond of glow and light chartreuse with air-clear water.

Also, never forget the classics. For years, the two go-to choices in soft plastics were strawberry with a white tail and root beer with a reddish orange tail. With topwaters, bone has been the stalwart and chrome was likely the first truly popular color when topwaters emerged along the Texas coast. These classic combinations and shades are classics for a reason. They consistently work. It is funny that you do not see those color patterns (particularly strawberry with white tail) used consistently now. As with a lot of classics, it is not the fish that evolved out of susceptibility to those baits. It is the angler.

Remember too that color patterns can get hot and cold. I vividly remember a period years ago when a red topwater was critical for producing trout in the Bolivar Pocket. This unique flat on the Gulf side of Galveston's North Jetty is this odd union of bay and Gulf that can be an incredible wadefishing spot throughout the summer. This particular summer, the fish noticeably preferred red topwaters. I have no clue why, but it really mattered as much as five-to-one, so I painted, dyed, and stained everything this side of my boat hull with red ink, fingernail polish, and paint. I had more red baits in my boxes and on my customers' lines than all other colors combined. It was a deadly pattern—until it wasn't. As quickly as that pattern emerged, it seemed to go the opposite direction, and I had painted and red markered every chrome bait I had. The pattern was real and I had to go with it, but ultimately, it reverted back. I believe the lesson in this is to be open to new designs, shades, and combinations for sure, but with limited space in any wading belt box and countless colors of tails, plugs, top-waters, and spoons available, stick to baits that you know consistently get results.

It's All about the Archer

I obviously like this image. As previously mentioned, there is a great line that marksmanship in archery is all about the archer and has little to do with the arrow. Obviously, you have to have a fairly good arrow to land your mark, but it is the archer who has the majority of the influence on what hits the target or not. In fishing, color selection will always matter, but confidence and skill always beat color. So, if you truly try to answer the question, "How do you combat the fact that color sometimes really matters?" the short answer is, "Don't." Stick to the basics that bring you the highest confidence factor. Focus on developing your angling skill and ability to pattern fish, and color selection will fade in importance (pun intended).

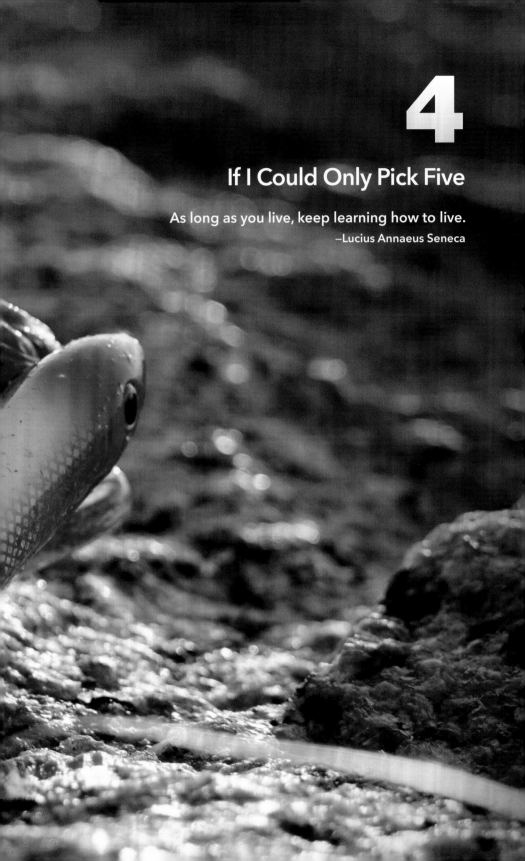

4

If I Could Only Pick Five

As long as you live, keep learning how to live.
—Lucius Annaeus Seneca

KEY POINTS

- You will note that most experts' picks allow them to cover a broad spectrum of needs, from water depth to a variety of types of feeding patterns.

- Never forget the classics.

- The next time you look at your lure box, think about what five baits you have the confidence to literally survive with for your entire fishing future. Think about why you would pick those. Is it that they have produced for you, or that you just know they have produced for others?

AS ANGLERS, we always want the proverbial silver bullet, and the lure choices of experts just feel superior. Like some type of "insider information," those baits must have an advantage. If he or she uses that bait, it has to work. Right?

There actually is some validity to this fantasy. Confidence is the key to sports, shooting, investing, speaking, and writing, and fishing is no different. An extra hint of confidence in a bait can lead to extra attention in working it and often allows a weary or frazzled angler to stick out a pattern, even if the bite is slow or nonexistent. As mentioned in

chapter 3, we have all had that feeling that "I must just be throwing the wrong lure," but a little confidence can change everything.

Honestly, beyond the proven bait types listed, there is some very good insight embedded in the scholarly selections listed in this chapter. You will note that with their modest selection of only five baits, these seasoned anglers all pick enough variance of bait style to address varying parts of the water column, a variety of feeding patterns, and various activity levels for trout and redfish. It is easy for anglers to get hung up in the rainbow of color choices, and often it is the bait's style, presentation, and action that are the actual attractant . . . or not. (Note Greg Stunz's observations in chapter 5.)

Among the themes, you may also notice that there is a consistent presence of some of the classic baits. Spoons are largely no different than the first ones crafted a century or maybe centuries ago. Remember that trout and redfish feeding impulses do not materially change through the years. Never forget the classics. They work.

Remember too that the quest for the best five baits is meant to focus your attention on addressing the key qualities needed for successful angling and to control your impulse from looking for the "magic" lure. This chapter is not meant to be a glimpse into a holy tackle box, but if you are like me, it does feel pretty darn close.

You will note that some lures have more detailed descriptions than others. I tried to keep them as consistent as possible, but there was some variance among the team of experts as to their exact descriptions of colors, inclusion of a jighead weight, and so forth. I stayed as true as possible to their original choices and descriptions.

Brian Holden

Brian is a full-time fishing and hunting guide in the Rockport area and was general manager of the legendary Redfish Lodge. (As an aside, Redfish Lodge was devastated by Hurricane Harvey.) Brian is the personification of focus and determination. His skill, intensity, and tenacity make him an incredibly consistent and successful guide. After sending me his list, he followed up with a middle-of-the-night edit that woke him up in terror for forgetting it. If that does not speak to his intensity and focus, I do not know what does.

- Paul Brown's Original Fat Boy in chartreuse
- Texas Trout Killer in pumpkinseed
- Gulp 3-inch mantis shrimp in new penny
- Hedden One Knocker in bone
- Down South Lures in "chicken of the C" pattern

Robert Taylor

Besides being CCA's national director of state development, Robert is an incredibly well-traveled and exceptionally talented angler. Among the many great anglers I have had the privilege to fish with and around, I would clearly put Robert in the best-of-breed category. The funny thing about Robert's fishing interests is the incredible diversity and range of fishing he does. He is no less comfortable throwing a grotesquely over-sized chugger for surfacing yellowfin tuna than dabbling a $\frac{1}{64}$-oz. buck jig for a crappie. It is all one continuum for Robert. I also have to note that Robert was likely the most tortured of all of those I asked to provide their best five lures. I finally had to tell him that I could not field any additional follow-up questions and simply needed his list. He begrudgingly posted his five but sent them with significant anguish that he could not add a supplemental Paul Brown's Original Twitchbait or 51-series MirrOlure. He was literally tortured by it.

- Heddon Super Spook Jr. in bone
- Bass Assassin 5-inch straight tail in plum with a $\frac{1}{16}$-oz. Norton jighead
- Bass Assassin Sea Shad in roach pattern with $\frac{1}{8}$-oz. Norton jighead
- Bass Assassin 5-inch straight tail in limetruese with a ¼-oz. Norton jighead
- ¼-oz. weedless silver spoon with a red trailer

Dr. Larry McKinney

Most Texans who love the outdoors know Larry's name, and if they do not, they should because they have benefitted from the accomplishments of his storied career in some way. Larry held a variety of leadership roles in Texas Parks and Wildlife Department, with the most notable being coastal fisheries director. He is currently the executive director of the Harte Research Institute at Texas A&M University Corpus Christi, helping lead some of the most cutting-edge marine science in the country. What most do not know about Larry is that he doesn't just manage and study trout and redfish; he aggressively pursues them with equal success. As featured in chapter 5, "Scientist Angler," Larry understands trout and redfish on a level that few do. I must note that he too begrudgingly conjured up his go-to conventional baits, but not due to the difficulty of culling to five choices. . . . He wanted to only list flies. I reminded him that these are supposed to be the baits you would live off of if you could only fish with five. Needless to say, he relinquished and provided five tested choices.

- Heddon Super Spook Jr. in bone
- Bagley Brite castin spoon ½-oz. in gold
- Berkley anchovy 6-inch Jerk Shad on an Owner twistlock 5/0 full gap hook
- Bass Assassin sea shad in pumpkinseed with chartreuse tail on a ⅛-oz. / 2/0 Sled Head
- DOA shrimp ½-oz. in green metal flake under a yellow Cajun Thunder cork

Joe Doggett

For a generation (or more) of Texas anglers, Joe Doggett's acclaimed writing has captured what it feels like to wade into a crystal surf or explore a back cove. Often, his creative depictions are as good as the real thing or, in some cases, may be even better. Along with his iconic status as an outdoor writer, Joe has literally fished the world and has experienced virtually every dimension of Texas bay angling. His five picks reflect his cosmopolitan approach to fishing with a truly old-school leaning.

- Johnson Sprite ½-oz. gold spoon (Joe did mention upgrading the hook and split ring.)
- Dixie Jet spoon ¾-oz. silver
- Norton Sand Eel Jr. in Pearl with chartreuse tail on a ¼-oz. jighead
- MirrOlure 51M in dark green with silver sides
- Rapala Skitter Walk in bone with silver sides

Doug Pike

A true multimedia communicator of all things outdoors, Doug is known for his years writing for newspapers, periodicals, and books, and his continued long run on Houston-area radio. Doug is as likely to be fishing for a speckled trout in Baffin Bay as a largemouth bass on Lake Fork. His experience and expertise have given him an ocean of insight into the best baits.

- Johnson Sprite ¾-oz. gold spoon
- Skitter Walk in speckled trout pattern
- MirrOlure C-Eye Pro Dog Jr. in BNSB pattern
- Paul Brown's Original Fat Boy in dayglow
- MirrOlure 51M808

Dr. Greg Stunz

Greg's scientific insight into speckled trout and redfish is possibly only transcended by his passion to catch them on rod and reel. Living in Port Aransas, Greg is able to pursue his love of fishing as well as his illustrious academic career as a professor at the Texas A&M University Corpus Christi Harte Research Institute and the director of the Center for Sportfish Science and Conservation. Greg is the classic scientist angler.

- Heddon Super Spook Jr. in okie shad pattern
- Paul Brown's Original Suspending Twitchbait in chartreuse
- MirrOdine in silver
- Texas Trout Killer 5-inch in brown with a chartreuse tail on a $\frac{1}{16}$-oz. Hogie springhead jig
- Johnson Sprite weedless spoon ¼-oz. in gold

James Fox

World explorers were metaphorically said to have a map of the world on their face. They pioneered new areas before anyone even thought to go there and cut dirt paths that are used as highways today. They literally break new ground. Along the middle Texas coast, that per-

fectly described the late James Fox. He was a guide before there really was a defined guiding business, and he built a clientele before it was widely thought possible to make a living guiding. Having the pleasure of knowing James for many years, he was an unending fountain of knowledge (among other choice insights and words) and will forever be a true legend along the Texas coast. His picks reflect his deep roots in Texas coastal angling.

- MirrOlure 51MR in Texas chicken pattern
- Johnson Sprite ½-oz. gold spoon
- Kelly Wiggler 4-inch shrimptail in strawberry with a white tail (I didn't actually know you could still buy a Kelly Wiggler anymore, so I really loved having it in this list. You can still buy them, now called Kwigglers, in many tackle stores.)
- Hedden Super Spook in bone
- Berkley Gulp! 4-in shrimptail in glow with a chartreuse tail

Chester Moore

Chester has never met a fish he didn't want to catch. Not unlike my references in Robert Taylor's brief bio, Chester is as versatile an angler as you will ever meet. He has his specialties, namely pursuing southern flounder, but is as comfortable fishing in an inland reservoir as around a deepwater Gulf of Mexico platform. Chester fishes, hunts, traps, skins, and does all things outdoors with an enthusiasm that is contagious. He is classically the guy who would win a survival contest and actually gain weight in the process. A true outdoorsman. His five baits reflect his willingness to target diverse patterns and his ability to explore the entire water column.

- Skitter Walk in trout pattern
- Gulp! swimming mullet in smoke pattern
- Johnson Sprite ¼-oz. silver spoon
- Sebile Splasher with clear belly and black back
- Egret Baits wedgetail mullet

Shannon Thompkins

Shannon is one of the most acclaimed and tenured newspaper outdoor writers along the Gulf. His literal decades of fishing experience come from his willingness to fish from the backwaters to the blue water. His ability to translate that experience and expertise to the outdoor en-

thusiasts of Texas and beyond has made him an award-winning icon in the outdoor writing space. Shannon's five baits reflect his undeniable old-school leaning (which I can relate to) and his willingness to fish unconventional baits.

- Rat-L-Trap in gold with black back (color code 143)
- Bass Assassin sea shad in pearl with a chartreuse tail and a wide-gap jighead
- Heddon Spit N' Image 3 ¼-inch model X9270 in threadfin shad pattern
- Storm Jointed ThunderStick in bone with a red belly
- MirrOlure 22MRCFPR Catch 2000 Jr. (with chartreuse back, pearl belly, and silver sides)

This eclectic group of current and past professional guides, outdoor writers, scientists, expert amateur anglers, and everything in between is meant to give you a view not only into the picks of the greats, but into the thinking and experience that framed those picks. The next time you look at your lure box, think about what five baits you could literally survive with for the rest of your days on the water. Think about why you would pick those. Is it that they have produced, or that you just know they have produced for others?

Ultimately, great anglers catch fish with different styles, sizes, and colors of baits because those baits fit their individual styles. If that was not the case, you would have just read identical lists of "best five picks." Additionally, I would speculate that if you asked the exact same experts who were polled for this chapter what their favorite five baits are right now as opposed to when I wrote this, they would likely answer with similar but different particular selections. (In full disclosure, having asked this question of some of these characters a number of times, their choices can change daily.) In the end, your best will come from finding the best five for you and your style. As you go through this process of analysis of what you think really is effective, you will likely find a new level of confidence and in turn a greater success rate.

5

The Scientist Angler

Progress is not achieved by luck or accident,
but by working on yourself daily.

–Epictetus

KEY POINTS

- Fish move more than people know. Speckled trout can range shockingly far distances in just a day.

- The ideas that fish travel in schools is a cliché for a reason. . . . they really do. Remember to plant your feet, drop your anchor, or mark your spot when you catch a fish. That fish may very well have a lot of schoolmates around it.

- Go fish. Remember that the only way you can catch fish is to actually go. Sound simple? Then go fish.

- Remember that fish do not feed all the time. Like all animals, they are not constantly on the bite. Just because you are not getting bites does not mean you are not on fish. Read the signs, and if you are confident, grind it out.

- Don't ignore the environmental clues as to what the fish are doing. It is very easy to apply the same retrieve, same lure selection, or go to the same spots regardless of the air and water conditions. Read the water and environment, and let that guide you in your choices.

- Fish have a "sixth sense" ability to sense vibration. Make sure you have some baits that have a hard rattle or vibration. Appealing to that sixth sense can open up your opportunities in off-color water and tough-bite situations.

IN AN ERA of the emergence of the angler scientist, where anglers are now participating in and promoting marine science, I was struck by a corollary to that in the scientist angler. More anglers are getting involved in the science of conservation by participating in tagging programs, catch-and-release technology, and data collection. Interestingly, there are some in the marine science community who have embraced that union of passions for decades. Angler scientists are undoubtedly invaluable for the marine science community, but maybe we need to remember we have a lot to learn from angler scientists as well.

The knowledge and insight of a marine biologist has always been incredibly alluring to me. I imagine most anglers feel a certain amount of curiosity and even envy when imagining that marine biologists might have a unique and cryptic piece of the secret formula for successful angling. Through the countless hours slaving away in florescent-lit laboratories, conducting exhaustive field work, sifting through piles of research and analysis, and generally dissecting all things in the marine world, they clearly know more about the biology of our beloved fish than we ever will.

Like some form of fish psychiatrists, they spend their days unraveling the most intricate and indiscernible mysteries involving the whys, wheres, and hows that drive fish. That has to be valuable to better angling. What Freudian slip makes a trout bite? What Jungian tendency makes a redfish and flounder move offshore to spawn? Do they have privacy issues? Did momma flounder coddle her kids too much, or was daddy redfish just too hard on his growing up? It just seems like marine biologists have the inside scoop.

I have to believe marine biologists have that all figured out, or at least I like to imagine they do.

With the lure of a scientific approach to Texas bay angling, I reached out to a number of different and diverse Texas-based biologists to capture their best tips to improve angling skills. All are true experts in their respective fields, but each one brings intriguingly different perspectives to their studies and to our development in the art of angling.

Larry McKinney

As highlighted in the previous chapter, Dr. McKinney has seen it all. From studying marine biology at Texas A&M University in the 1970s to heading the Coastal Fisheries Division for the Texas Parks and Wildlife Department, he has both studied and helped manage many of the fish we love the most. In his off time, he frequently kayaks the flats of Texas' middle coast with fly rod (and occasionally conventional tackle) in hand. When asked about his most surprising observation on the patterns of fish, his insight reveals a critical clue.

"Fish move much more than people could ever imagine," said Dr. McKinney. "It goes against everything my dad ever taught me. He always believed that you go to the spot, and the fish are simply going to be there. Tagging studies have shown that species like speckled trout move tremendous distances. You may pull into your favorite spot and the fish from the prior day or even prior tide may be long gone . . . and may never return. Other fish may replace them, but you have to remember that fish have those fins for a reason."

Shane Bonnot

Shane is as much a scientist as an advocate. As the advocacy director for CCA Texas, he spends his work days dealing with Texas Parks and Wildlife Department (TPWD), the TPWD Commission, the Texas Legislature, and every other managing agency, including the Texas Commission on Environmental Quality, General Land Office, and the array of river authorities that all affect our experience as recreational anglers. Prior to coming to CCA, Shane was a hatchery manager at the revered Sea Center Texas hatchery in Lake Jackson, Texas. He oversaw the production of some of Texas anglers' favored species, and if you are an angler who regularly targets redfish, speckled trout, and southern flounder, you may very well have had the honor of catching a fish that Shane helped raise.

As familiar as Shane is with a scientific lab and the halls of the Texas Capitol, he is just as comfortable fishing his home waters in the Matagorda Bay Complex. He is an avid light tackle angler and has logged enough hours to have a truly seasoned résumé. When asked about the most useful takeaway for anglers that he has gleaned from his years at the hatchery, he quickly responded:

> As anglers, we often forget that "school of fish" is not a cliché. Trout, redfish, and particularly flounder can travel in shockingly tight schools. I think most fisherman underestimate the degree to which fish will school. You can easily witness this in a hatchery setting. At Sea Center Texas, there are two twenty-foot diameter tanks that are used for spawning flounder broodstock. Each tank is stocked with approximately eighty fish, which may seem like a lot of fish in one tank, but in that space there is plenty of room for the fish to spread out. It is amazing to see how many fish will congregate in one area and bed up on one another, leaving some large areas of the tank void of fish. Our human instinct is to think that they would like to have some space and spread out to lay down on the tank floor, bay bottom, or sea bed. Not the case at all with flounder.

There is an important lesson in Shane's words. It is very easy to forget the schooling nature of fish, and in the excitement of locating a school and getting a bite or two, we often mindlessly wade or drift through the fish without thoroughly fishing the area. On your next wade or

drift trip, remember to plant your feet or hit a MOB marker on your GPS when you get a bite. You may find that a bite can quickly turn into a school.

Robin Riechers

Robin is the Coastal Fisheries director for the Texas Parks and Wildlife Department. This translates into a classically nonstop job that spans from dealing with the most intricate science of fish to the most contentious politics of fish found at the Texas Capitol and federal fishery management system. Robin eats, sleeps, and breathes coastal fisheries and is keenly attuned to stock assessments, hatchery production, coastal economics, and everything that creates, impacts, and touches the coastal fisheries ecosystem both literally and figuratively.

He does not get to fish nearly as much as he would like, but after more than twenty-nine years working for TPWD in a variety of positions, he has a unique insight into both fish and fishermen.

"As someone who spends much of his time looking at and reviewing data and talking about fishery policy issues as opposed to actually getting to fish, the old adage that comes to mind is if you actually go fishing you are going to catch a lot more fish."

The irony of fishermen is that they have so much passion for the art of fishing but spend incalculably more time and money on preparing to, thinking about, and dreaming of fishing rather than actually fishing. I love Robin's point. Go fish. (See chapter 12 for a further bout of preaching on this important subject.)

Joan Holt

Dr. Holt is a living legend along the Texas coast. Her years of study and instruction at the University of Texas Marine Science Institute (UTMSI) have fundamentally changed the face of marine biology. She is as storied and acclaimed as she is passionate about marine biology and the coastal environment where she lives, studies, teaches, and (of course) fishes.

Years spent tank-side tending to all makes and models of finfish have taught her a lot about feeding patterns. Her observations regarding the odd-looking and often-mysterious southern flounder reveal an important fact for anglers.

"Anglers tend to often assume that if they are not catching fish, the fish are simply not there. That could not be farther from the truth," warns Dr. Holt. "Southern flounder are particularly disciplined in their feeding patterns. When hungry, they will literally swim to the top of the tank to be nearly hand fed. When not feeding, you can place any form of food in front of them, and they will not budge."

As an aside, a grad student at UTMSI once recounted to me a story of watching a live shrimp gingerly walk across the face of a resting flounder without harm. That stunning imagery highlights Dr. Holt's point that fish can be as particular and finicky about their feeding times as we humans are. Just because there is a steak in front of you does not mean you are going to eat it. Additionally, an important takeaway is that just because you do not get a bite does not mean you are not on a school of fish. It is extremely easy to assume that you are in dead water if you are not catching anything. Remember that finding fish can often be just a small part of the journey to a successful fishing trip.

Robert Vega

Now retired, Dr. Vega previously directed one of the largest marine finfish hatchery programs in the world. The TPWD marine hatcheries focus primarily on rearing speckled trout, red drum, and southern flounder, but their research reaches far beyond our beloved big three species. Robert is a pure scientist, and in his past role as enhancement director of the Coastal Fisheries Hatchery Program, which includes the Flour Bluff CCA Marine Development Center, Sea Center Texas, and the Perry R. Bass Marine Fisheries Station, he helped produce millions and millions of fish every year. This unique day job of fish creation provided an eerily intimate insight into the minds of fish. Think about it . . . Dr. Vega literally made trout, redfish, and flounder. It is as inspiring a pursuit as it is a touch creepy.

Although an angler, he would never call himself an expert in fishing, but for this exploration, that is merely a caveat. When asked how we as aspiring anglers could better understand the role of patterning trout and redfish, Dr. Vega notes the critical part that water temperature and salinity play in the patterns of all species of coastal finfish.

"Each species is unique in its wants and needs regarding temperature, salinity, and habitat," advises Dr. Vega. "These critical environmental features control all aspects of life, including spawning, seasonal migrations, growth, and feeding."

Dr. Vega's observation comes from years of being immersed in the lives of the finfish species that are important to us, and his input speaks to a key component to successful angling: be observant of the environment you are fishing. You have to be a student of the fish and environment in which they dwell. Virtually every pattern has some tie to an environmental underpinning. Remember to be adaptive and observant in defining fish patterns. As the saying goes, they change as often as the weather. Also, study the species you pursue. There is something that drives them uniquely in many of their seasonal and daily patterns. The better you know these motivations, the more you will intercept them.

Greg Stunz

Dr. Stunz is a common reference throughout this book and in many of my other writings and photography. His expertise as an angler is only outpaced by his renown abilities as a marine scientist at Texas A&M University's Harte Research Institute and Center for Sportfish Science and Conservation. He is also a regular on Discovery Channel's *Shark Week* (which has little to do with coastal trout and redfish fishing, but makes him particularly cool).

From the convenient sling of his backyard boat dock, Greg regularly fishes the bays and flats of Texas' middle coast. He is a hardcore wade fisherman, who is as comfortable stalking a grass flat as analyzing a finfish stock assessment. His years in the lab, teaching, conducting field work, and doing extensive tagging studies on some of our sport's most revered sportfish, make him an expert's expert. When quizzed on the single most important insight that he has gleaned from his scientific work that he regularly uses in his angling efforts, Dr. Stunz says:

> A key to catching more fish is appealing to the "sixth sense" fish have in their lateral line. They can use this intricate sensory organ that runs the length of their body to assess their environment in a way humans have little ability to imagine. They have a distant touch and regularly use it to make themselves more effective in capturing prey. The tip here is to make sure you incorporate baits that create vibration and do not be afraid to fish turbid, murky water. As a matter of fact, I suggest that many times you should seek out lower visibility water.

Greg's point is a great reminder that a bait's color can matter far less than its ability to vibrate and rattle. Additionally, he reminds us that our natural default of looking for the clearest water can be a mistake. If you think about it, the clarity actually gives the predator a significant disadvantage in pursuing his prey. The next time you approach a reef or shoreline that has baitfish present, but the water is disappointingly dismal, give it a wade or drift and use a deep-rattle topwater or big-vibration spoon. You might find your own secret pattern.

Back to School

One of the timeless beauties of angling is that you are never done learning. Every day on the water, every conversation with a fellow angler, and every article you read help refine your art. The best angling and life advice I ever received was to never stop learning, and I think to properly do that, you have to never stop looking for new and different sources. Marine biologists, fishery managers, and everyone in between are always pushing their science and their art. They constantly stretch to increase our shared understanding of the marine resources we all adore. Don't ignore that research. While there is no scientific formula for angling success, adding a little marine biology to your tackle box will clearly increase your odds.

6

Hiring A Pro

There are always new places to go fishing. For any fisherman, there's always a new place, always a new horizon.
–Jack Nicklaus

KEY POINTS

- Pick your guide carefully. Make sure you decide if you want to fish with bait or lure. Neither style is better or worse, but they are very different approaches and often require a different type of guide. Be honest with yourself and your guide about your skill level and personal expectations, and you will both have a better trip.

- The same holds true for wading or drifting/anchoring. The best approach is to be flexible, but make sure you are honest. If you are uncomfortable wading, your guide needs to know well in advance of the trip's departure.

- Make sure you reflect on the real reason you are hiring a guide. Is it for a client thank you? Do you want to learn new spots? Do you just want to get out and fish stress-free? None of these are bad objectives, but your guide needs to know the general objective of the trip so he or she can have the insight needed to cater to your intended purpose.

I HAVE TO profess my bias for the value of fishing guides. The good ones are simply priceless. Although there are plenty who do not put their heart into it, once you are around one who does, you cannot deny the incredible potential for learning that comes in just a single day of fishing with them.

Having been a guide many years ago and now having the pleasure to occasionally fish with a few of them, I have been fortunate to truly see the experience from both sides. I can promise you that the good ones are unimaginably determined, not just to find fish but to enable you to actually catch them. They go to sleep thinking about fish patterns, and they wake up on fire to get to the ramp. They wear out their bodies and compete against their peers and themselves every single day. They are willing to trailer their boat across the coast to capitalize on emerging and sometimes divergent patterns, and look at trailer tires and wheel bearings as an expendable and necessary casualty of their driven pursuit. They are unapologetically intense.

The great thing about the guiding arena is that anyone can get a chance to book a day with the true superstars of coastal fishing. Good luck getting a pitching lesson from an MLB pitcher or a golf lesson from the winner of the US Open. But, if you are willing to make the financial commitment and plan ahead enough to get on their often-stuffed calendars, you can fish with the absolute best in the field of coastal fishing. It is a unique opportunity to accelerate the level of your art, but the key to having a truly productive guide experience is making sure you hire the right one for you and your group. This really does not take a lot of soul searching and deep reflection, but there are a number of key questions you can ask yourself and a prospect guide to ensure that you end up with the experience you really want.

Bait or Lure?

It's a simple question, but one that clients often do not address with true honesty. You have to remember that bait fishing and lure fishing are often dramatically different pursuits with equally divergent patterns attached to them. Additionally, guides are usually very attached to utilizing one style or the other. There are some who float fairly comfortably between the two disciplines, but you will commonly find that lure guides are lure guides and bait guides are bait guides. One is not better nor more skilled than the other—just different.

Make sure you know which one you truly want. If you really are indifferent as to which you use, ask the guide exactly what type of bait

fishing or lure fishing he or she commonly employs and what species are targeted. This will give you a gauge if you are likely to anchor at the jetties and freeline live shrimp for trout or wade a shallow back lake for redfish. Both examples can be fun but are very different experiences.

Wade or Drift?

Again, this is not a hard question but one that clients commonly neglect. Ultimately, its answer is critical to the success of the trip. If you or anyone in your group does not or cannot wade, you have to let your guide know. Additionally, I highly recommend that all members of the party go with one method or another. For safety reasons, most guides will not let you split up your group and drop off some anglers on a shoreline while some drift, but even if they do allow it, I wouldn't. Beyond the obvious problems that can emerge if someone on a shoreline or flat gets into a health crisis or is hit by a stingray, it also tends to diminish the guide's effectiveness in tracking fish. The best results usually come from the entire party focusing on the pattern the guide has determined will work the best. You essentially work as a team on a drift or wade in deciphering the details of the pattern. Separating the group can often work against the greater focus of finding the bite.

Additionally, ensuring that you and your guide understand the leanings of the group will allow him or her to get the needed current information to find fish. If the guide has not been on a drift pattern, they can likely get the needed information either from their years of experience or from their colleagues. The worst scenario is for a guide to be dialed into a phenomenal wading pattern and find out at the boat ramp that morning that the group cannot wade. In those cases, the odds for disappointment go up significantly.

The best approach is for the entire party to be adaptable and properly geared for wade or drift. That will allow the guide to capitalize on all of the insight he or she has and singularly focus on producing a quality experience.

What Is the Real Goal of the Trip?

There are a lot of tremendous reasons to hire a guide, including learning a new bay, sharpening your skills, client cultivation, or even a bag

of fillets (which is likely the worst ratio of dollars to pounds for fish you might ever find). The only bad answer to this pivotal question comes when you are not honest with yourself.

I clearly remember having an occasional trip during late fall and winter when a customer wanted to go grind a back bay shoreline or cove in the hope of getting a trophy trout. Sometimes they legitimately wanted to do that. Often, they liked the concept but really didn't want to invest the time and effort. What starts as a determined safari for a trophy gets blunted by punch-through, posthole-digging wades in thick mud and torturously repetitive casts with no bites. The hardcore never look up from wades like this, and can even derive true hope and enthusiasm from the faintest hint of baitfish on the shoreline. In contrast, those who only thought they wanted to grind quickly start small talk about drifting midbay reefs and reflect on that beloved trip last year when they fished schooling trout under birds. The trip generally goes downhill from there.

Make sure you know what you want for your trip. Odds are that you will plan it well in advance, and it will be a much-anticipated luxury. Ensure you have your expectations correctly grounded. There are countless variables in a guided trip, and the only thing your guide can guarantee is that they will try their hardest to get you on the water and on fish—but even that is impossible to guarantee. Veteran guide James Plaag (who may have the fastest wit of any on the bay) once quipped to a client who asked if they were going to catch limits that day, "I can't guarantee you that my motor will start; how can I guarantee you a limit?" No statement could be more accurate. Plaag is truly one of the best, but even the most-gifted guide doesn't have omnipotent power over all of the diverse variables that go into a day of fishing. Set your sights clearly, and go with the flow of your trip. If you do, it may be the best money you spend all year.

Get to Know Your Guide

This section is not specifically framed around a question but speaks to one of the most critical parts of having a good experience—"Will I like my guide?" We have all either heard stories of or even experienced a trip with an abrasive or dictatorial guide. From getting screamed at for missing a fish to getting lectured about the virtues of the guide's religious faith, the stories are common and often true. There is no guarantee that your guide will not Jekyll and Hyde on you, but there are a few steps you can take to get to know them in advance of booking your trip.

Try attending several seminars from guides who fish in the area you want to go. There are a number of venues for these often-intimate talks, including trade shows, local CCA chapters, and area fishing tackle stores and clubs. Many guides give talks to cultivate bookings and promote their gear sponsors, and in these settings, you get a chance to hear your prospective guide speak about their vision for fishing and answer questions regarding all things fishing. Generally, after thirty minutes to an hour, you will have a legitimate feel for his or her personality.

Through the years, I regularly heard from clients that they decided to book their trip from attending one of my seminars. This was not due to any gifted speaking prowess, but rather, they got a feel that I was informed, focused, and very much a student of the art of fishing. If that was what they wanted, it was an easy fit. If it wasn't, they went elsewhere. Additionally, in my experience, I've found that seminars regularly yielded my best clients. We started the trip already having a feel for each other, and it led to a much better exchange from the advent of the trip.

If you are targeting a guide who does not regularly give talks or is difficult to catch in person, make sure you have a thoughtful phone conversation with them. Most serious guides are relatively pressed for their evening phone time, but take a moment to ask more than the price of the trip and the everyday details. Ask them to recount a recent trip, and dig into their favorite fishing style. Even ask them about what types of trips their best clients tend to book. This will reveal the strengths and fishing style of the guide and should allow you to determine if you want to get on their calendar.

Ultimately, hiring a pro is a great choice for anyone aspiring to improve their skills, and by honestly asking yourself what you want out of the trip, the odds are high that you will get more knowledge and insight than you even imagined.

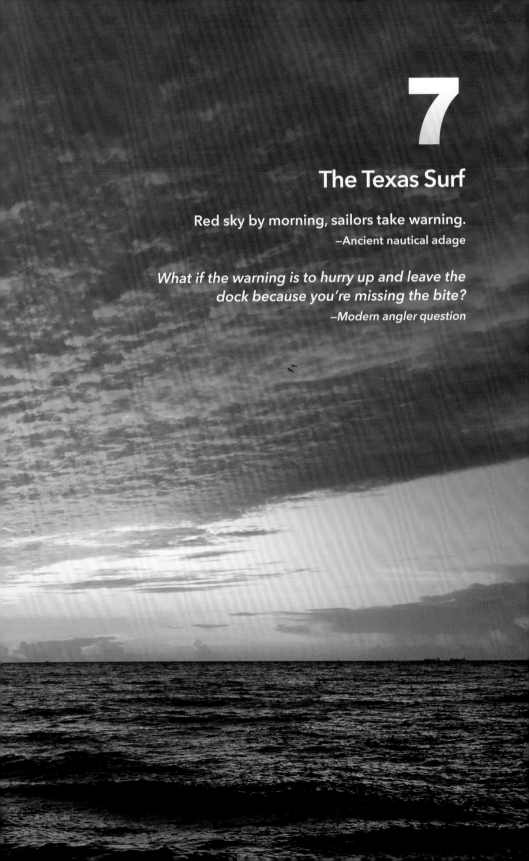

7

The Texas Surf

Red sky by morning, sailors take warning.
—Ancient nautical adage

*What if the warning is to hurry up and leave the
dock because you're missing the bite?*
—Modern angler question

KEY POINTS

- Find a surf cam for your area. Many popular beaches have surf cameras that allow feeds of video or still photos of the beach conditions. A surf cam is an invaluable tool for real-time water conditions.

- Go light. The less gear you take often results in the best experience in the surf. Outfit yourself with all of the necessities, but don't overload. Efficiency is your friend in the surf.

- Look for any abnormalities in the pattern of the surf. Even the slightest variance can serve as an ambush spot for gamefish.

- Don't wait for perfect conditions to fish the surf. The fish are not as sensitive to water clarity as we anglers are. "Trout green water" is great to have . . . but not imperative.

- Safety is key in any surf trip. Invest in a life vest and remember to expect the unexpected when wading the surf.

FEW MORNINGS in Texas saltwater fishing come with more anticipation than the first fishable, warm tides of early summer along the Texas coast. Hunters have the season opener of dove, turkey, deer, and a number of other beloved species, but there is no season that brings more exciting opportunity and allows even we who are boatless to experience truly world-class speckled trout fishing in one of the most breathtaking settings in coastal angling.

Fishing the surf for trout has always been a passion for me but has elevated to a distracting obsession in the past decade. It has always held great mystery and appeal, dating back to early memories of horrifically sandy, hot, dehydrating (but strangely alluring) camping trips to San Luis Pass as a child. Most trips ending in some form of mechanical disaster, rashes, injury, and very few fish, but I couldn't wait to go back. I knew that the next time we were going to have an epic catch . . . next time. I literally dreamed about it. I actually once asked Santa for a beach camping trip. (You know my dad cringed when he read my list of wants that year.) Those trips to the edge of the ocean forever tattooed the power and lure of the Texas surf on me. It's still there.

Nowhere outside the surf does a traditional bay angler have such potential to encounter anything from a fiery speckled trout to a world-class tarpon. Honestly, I have likely seen more amazing glimpses of the ocean's power on the Galveston beachfront than anywhere else in my travels as an angler. That may seem like hyperbole, but when you consider the shadows of upsettingly giant sharks, an occasional free-vaulting king mackerel, and airborne spinner sharks in the sunrise, it's hard to imagine a more diverse carnival of activity than the surf. It's literally addictive.

The surf holds so many important ingredients for an angler. With surprisingly abundant access from public parking areas and seemingly endless stretches to wade if you are willing to walk a bit farther, the choices can be a bit overwhelming.

With the privatization of so much of Texas' land, the surf is one of the last sprawling and somewhat untamed stretches of outdoor access. Although driving the length of the beach is precluded in many areas, the access still far outstrips many if not all bay systems along the entire Texas coast. And you not only don't need a boat; I honestly believe it is far better pursued without a boat in many instances. When I was still fishing with customers and felt the need to guide them via boat rather than meeting them at the beach, I found the flexibility of having a boat for mobility at times led me to spend too much time looking and not enough focusing on the basics needed to pattern the surf.

I have pursued numerous species in the Texas surf, but the overwhelming majority of my focus has been on wadefishing for speckled trout with artificial lures. It encapsulates one of the purest and most uncluttered trout fishing experiences. By applying a simple and sometimes unconventional approach to surf fishing for trout, I believe it can become any angler's favorite summertime passion.

The Surf Cam

I would put the inventor of the surf cam (beachfront-mounted cameras that stream video or successive still shots of surf conditions) in the same illustrious category as the genius that first put wheels on a piece of heavy luggage or molded plastic to form the first cooler. It is pure genius. Growing up relying on wind reports and often-suspect water condition reports from beachfront piers (not to say they would lie to get you to drive down there . . .), it was revolutionary to be able to simply go to your computer and get a real-time view of the surf size and relative color. It actually can become addictive. I hazard to think of the collective work hours lost across the Texas coast starting in May of every year due to computer-driven glimpses and resulting slack-jawed stares at a slow-rolling green surf.

The unprecedented value of the surf cam is that it can allow you to see the water you will likely be facing, but you must also remember that conditions can change through a night. If you are trying to participate in the dawn patrol, the water can change dramatically, sometimes with little to no change in surf size. The surf cam is a great guide, but remember that no indicator is perfect. I have departed my early morning perch in Houston with the highest of optimism, only to arrive on the Galveston beachfront and find conditions that are much deteriorated if not unfishable. But, I must caveat, there have been a number of occasions when I went ahead and waded into a rising surf or disappointingly diminished (or even poor) water clarity only to find a robust bite. Ultimately, use the camera's feed as a guide and know that everything is subject to change.

Keeping It Simple

The first step to a successful surf wading trip is to keep it simple. By nature, anglers want to overcomplicate and overgear every situation. The surf wading experience is progressively and exponentially diminished by every incremental increase in the amount of gear that adorns you. My absolute favorite wade is slipping into the surf at first light clad in a hooded shirt, long wading pants, neoprene boots, a rod and reel, a simple wading belt with pliers (and a lanyard for the inevitable times you will drop them), and a basic lure box, with no additional gear. If you plan to keep fish, you will need a long stringer (ten to fifteen feet) or a donut-style floating ring and mesh basket. I'm all for keeping fish if they are within legal limits and are going to be utilized, but it is a liberating experience to fish the surf without the nag of a stringer. Try it. It is a very different experience.

Your choice of lures should be equally spartan. I stick with a few topwaters. I'm particularly confident with a white body/red head Heddon Super Spook Jr. (I have really gotten into this bait in the past few years) and a chartreuse back and belly Super Spook. Having a couple of ¼-oz.

silver spoons is a must, but know that if you are like me and not a huge fan of leaders, you are going to lose some spoons to mackerel and juvenile bluefish. It is critical to have a couple of 51M-series Mirr-O-Lures. This bait was made for the surf and has a reputation for being able to rapidly cover water and can result in jarring strikes that rival few other applications. You can fire it into an onshore wind, and I must admit that it produces one of my favorite bites in all of fishing. Working a MirrOlure during an aggressive feeding period definitely plays to the hunter-stalker in all of us. It's the kind of strike that will wake you up later that night. I cannot imagine wading into the surf without a 51MCHG. The other classics for me are the 51M28 and 51MHP. You also need to pack a few jigs, but I keep it incredibly simple. I bring a few light and dark shades, primarily Bass Assassin straight tails in plum, pumpkinseed with chartreuse tail, and glow with chartreuse tail. That will allow you to cover a number of water conditions and will model most of the prey the trout are pursuing. I bring ¹⁄₁₆-, ¹⁄₈-, and ¼-oz. jigheads. The wind and wave action require some flexibility in jighead size, but don't be afraid to use the lightest possible jighead weight. It is easy to think that with the wind and current of the beachfront you want a heavy jighead, but the same rules apply in the surf as anywhere—fish often prefer a slow-falling bait, particularly when they are not feeding aggressively.

Look for the Unusual

If you visualize the crescent of the Texas coast, it gives you a scope as to the way fish travel along its rim. The series of tide-sculpted bars and guts create natural highways for all species to travel and hunt, and allows fish to travel incredible distances in short spans of time. Through his acoustic tracking network, Dr. Greg Stunz has recorded trout traveling unimaginable distances in a matter of days. Although not the norm, they can travel between passes like we drive between interstate cities. It is shocking. With that mind, finding the exceptions to this seemingly monotonous highway of structure is the difference between wandering into an occasional school of trout and actually patterning fish in the surf.

The keys to finding sweet spots in the surf are keeping your eyes open and getting your feet wet. You have to explore to discover the patterns. The majority of surf waders simply pick a convenient spot, blindly step into the water, and wade along on the same bar, for the same distance, and never explore. It's human nature and undoubtedly a bad call. One of the best patterns I ever found in the surf came one morning I had caught few fish but had made a painfully long wade on Galveston's east beach. The surf's wave action was beginning to pick up through the midmorning, and about a half mile from my parking spot, I started to notice that there was one stretch where the wave action was different. There seemed to be odd spacing between the crested waves. It had the look of waves going over a flat more than a normal short bar. I noted it, and the next calm morning that I was able to fish, I started in that spot. I quickly discovered that for some reason the bars were configured differently in that area. The waves broke seemingly longer because the space between guts was modestly larger. That area outproduced anything I had fished in the surf for several years before eventually disappearing. The proverbial sands of time eroded, and now it is contiguous, but it taught me a valuable lesson: In areas of vast, contiguous structure, look for any anomalies. The simple fact is that the predators that we are pursuing are playing off those very same anomalies to ambush their prey. If you find a variance in the continuity of structure (which actually applies to jetties and reefs just as readily), make sure and exploit it. It likely is a great spot.

The Myth of Trout-Green Water

This section is not meant as a diminishment of the productivity of the legend of trout-green water. It floods the beach through maddeningly few days during a summer, but when light northerly or southeasterly winds and tides cooperate, it creates a calm clarity that is zen-like for the beach fishing wannabe. It is undoubtedly a productive circum-stance, but it also is considered far too much of a guarantee of a good catch. I have caught a lot of trout in that magic mix of green clarity, but I have also had a stunning number of great days in water that, upon approach, appears sandy. The surf can be very deceptive. It can appear quite sandy, and when you wade in, you discover that it has an abundance of suspended sand but still has plenty of clarity. Honestly, I learned this from bleary mornings after making the early drive to the surf only to see the daunting salute of bayside flags and banners. At that point of being committed to the trip, I went ahead and tried a quick wade, knowing that a conciliatory Starbucks was a short truck ride away if it all went wrong. Again, catching fish in an off-color surf is not a consistent pattern, but it is worth a try more times than likely any of us give it.

I vividly remember a morning wading Galveston's seawall in what turned out to be truly sandy water. This was not the suspended sand look I referenced above. This was dead-up sandy. I had not had many mornings to fish the beach that year, and the wind was a light south, so I committed. As I strolled the second bar catching absolutely noth-ing, the glimmer of a slick in the first gut alerted me to a previously indistinguishable bait line that I had thoroughly ignored. I got inside on the bait line, switched to a full-size Super Spook, and the combi-nation of the large silhouette and loud rattle worked. To me, this was more rewarding than catching fish on a pristine classic surf morning, but more importantly, it taught me that the fish we desire catching in the surf likely often stay even if the conditions deteriorate. It is a failed instinct to believe that sandy water means the fish disperse. At times, that is probably true, but if the fish can stay on bait and have a feeding opportunity, there is likely no reason to move. I believe the lesson in this is to remember to not always try to fit the fish into the patterns we have established in our minds. They tend to have patterns of their own.

The polar opposite of the sandy water pattern is the phenomenon of poor fishing during long periods of perfect conditions. This pattern tends to emerge as the wind stabilizes for long stretches, particularly during late summer, and the surf becomes almost stagnant. The water can slack into a sterile air-clear and the bite becomes elusive. The schools of trout break up, and the surf tends to fill with all of the transient predators like Spanish mackerel, bluefish, juvenile jack crevalle, and a host of other bait biters. Additionally, those who choose to freeline live shrimp and particularly live croakers will generally outproduce lures significantly . . . sometimes to a disheartening degree for those wed to lures. The only break from this pattern is a disruption of increased wind that will aerate the surf and reshuffle the deck. At that point, the best plan is to wait for the conditions to settle, and the first two to three days of calm will again tend to yield strong results.

Know Your Limits

It would be irresponsible to write about wadefishing the surf without a significant word of caution. All of the potential trappings of wade-fishing anywhere are amplified in the surf. The exciting and limitless nature of the surf with its big horizon and open ocean ushers with it rip currents, undertows, rays, nasty jellyfish, and a host of other threats. This should not preclude a generally healthy individual from going, but one should always do so with a strong measure of caution.

The most important thing is to purchase a quality personal flotation device. There are no more excuses now that there are designs that are as sleek as any wading vest. There are choices that are unencumbering and provide the protection needed if you face rough conditions, the jolt of a ray spike, or some personal health emergency that impedes your ability to swim. It's a simple choice that is a true lifesaver.

Although it is not always practical, wading with a fishing buddy or two is advisable. It is definitely safer when traveling in a group. Not only does it help in locating fish and unraveling difficult feeding patterns; a group of anglers can rally far more effectively to address a life-and-death need than a solo angler.

My final warning is about the fabled third bar. For years, it has been a place of heralded myth. It is that last depot of sand that the tall and daring can perch on that allows fishing access into the abyss of the surf. It is a place of legends but can be a deceptively long swim from the second bar that can be extremely dangerous. I strongly caution against it. Honestly, most of the great fishing happens from the second bar, and I have found the third bar to lend itself to as many Herculean-sized skipjack as speckled trout. It would be dishonest for me to write that I had not had some tremendous catches from the third bar, but I honestly cannot remember the last time I swam out to find its elusive ridge. For me, it's easy to pass. The surf is an exciting and almost mystical place to fish—just make sure the excitement doesn't get you carried away . . . literally.

8

Five Ways to Make Yourself a Better Angler Today

The gods do not deduct from man's allotted span the hours spent in fishing.

–Herbert Hoover

KEY POINTS

- Make sure you have a well-fit and comfortable set (or sets) of polarized sunglasses. Outside of your rod and reel, it is the most important gear you have.

- Go with a guide. Experts never stop learning, and in angling, going with a guide is a tremendous way to continue learning (see chapter 6).

- Try a new bay. We all get locked in patterns. Dedicate yourself to fishing a few new bodies of water this year, and you will likely become a better all-around angler in the ones you already fish.

- Start a logbook. Keep it simple but be diligent about recording the basic details about where you succeeded and failed.

- Tune up your gear. You must have functioning tools to become a master craftsman. Replace your line. Ensure your reels are clean. Sharpen any old hooks. The key is taking the time to actually do it.

IN AN ERA filled with magazines, websites, podcasts, blog posts, and every other means of communication touting the next transformative career booster, life-preserving superfood, and even magic means to make you a better parent, I thought I would offer five simple and relatively cheap ways to make yourself a better angler. When I was fish guiding and even today fishing purely recreationally, I am always surprised to see very serious anglers show up for a fishing trip that they have anticipated for weeks or even months, having neglected some of the truly basic things that can dramatically improve a day fishing. There are likely countless other suggestions that we all can benefit from, but these are common and simple ones that can be implemented almost immediately.

New Sunglasses

I can still vividly remember my first pair of polarized sunglasses. It was a pair of Bill Dance Strike King glasses that literally covered a solid two-thirds of my face. The lenses were flat and massive, and the

thin metal frames adorned my face like a giant, flat, reflective billboard. They offered no wind protection and allowed enough glare to necessitate near-constant squinting, even with the glasses firmly in place. They likely would have been better for channeling the sun's power to start a fire or burn an anthill than they served for protecting my eyes or penetrating the water's surface, but at that time, they were state-of-the-art. When I first peered into the water with them, I thought I had found the window into the unseen kingdom. I could see bass beds in ponds, grasslines on bay flats, and an occasional fish silhouette (or at least I thought so) on a clear sandbar. It was pure magic to me.

Things have changed dramatically since then. Sunglasses technology has improved in every way. You can choose from a large variety of brand names with a shockingly broad range of prices, but most importantly, even the cheaper models are very good. Although not what I would suggest buying, I saw a $19 pair of convenience store polarized glasses in a rack while buying ice for a recent fishing trip that were better than my beloved Strike King monoliths. The simple fact is that, outside of our rod and reel, there likely is no more important physical component for the success of a fishing trip. Your sunglasses are your window to the signs that you need to locate and catch fish. There really is no excuse for not getting a good pair of glasses, and if you have a pair that are scratched, stretched, or otherwise significantly dilapidated, get a new pair. You will not regret it.

I have long used the Costa brand. There are a number of other great brands, but I love Costa's designs, durability, and their incredibly dedicated social mission. Their collective contribution to the marine conservation space is staggering. They have been longtime supporters of a number of nonprofit marine conservation groups and promote a multitude of high-impact conservation efforts on state, national, and international levels. They make a difference.

Make sure you check out several frame styles. Everyone's face is different, and it is critically important that your glasses fit your face to reduce wind penetration and sun glare while still giving you a wide screen for seeing the water. For me, the lighter the frames, the better. It may be psychological, but I feel so much less eye fatigue with light, tight frames. They stop the draining impact of wind and glare and, most importantly, don't weigh down your face through a long day of fishing.

There are an increasing number of shades of lens colors. For years, I adamantly adhered to a gray lens, believing it provided the greatest reduction of surface glare. Fishing the relatively murky waters of the Galveston Bay complex, I wanted a lens that heightened my ability to see slicks, birds, bait, and all surface-based signs more than a vermillion or yellow lens that is exceptional at penetrating the water for seeing fish silhouettes and subsurface structure. Through fishing a far-greater range of waters along the Texas coast and beyond, I now opt for a vermillion or reddish lens as my default.

The final piece in your glasses choice is the lanyard system you select to ensure you do not launch your new frames into the water. This may seem somewhat insignificant, but it is an important component. Not unlike frame selection, everyone is different, so try different brands and styles. I like a pair of holders that are particularly thin and have a very low profile where they attach to the back of the glasses' arms. My ears already stick out laughably far, so I really don't need anything to make them more winglike. That may seem irrelevant, but you need your glasses to feel like a part of you. You do not want them to become a distraction.

The best way to make the right choice of sunglasses is to take a moment and go to an outdoor products store that has a wide selection. Be the annoying guy or gal who gets a customer service person to allow you to try on . . . well . . . an annoying number of sunglasses frames. Make the right choice, and it will literally make you a better fisherman that day. Ultimately, there are not that many pieces of gear that can have such a fundamental impact, so there is no reason to not improve your angling eyes immediately.

Go with a Guide

I won't belabor this topic since I have dedicated an entire chapter to it, but hiring a guide is a crucial part of improving even the most experienced and expert angler's skills. Think about it—professional baseball players hire batting coaches. The world's best photographers, chefs, and so forth not only teach seminars; they attend them as well. Angling is no different. I have the privilege of fishing with a guide from time to time, and I never fail to learn something. It might be a new bait, technique, or even some technology that is completely foreign to me, but invariably there is something that increases my odds of locating and catching fish. Although a guide is an expensive luxury, split among a few friends, it is a worthy investment that will yield immediate returns.

Download a Map to a Bay You Have Never Fished

Download a new map to a bay that you have never fished. Oh yeah . . . and you have to actually go fish it. We are all creatures of habit. Honestly, we are not a lot different than the predators we try to catch in a day of fishing. We all have patterns of our own, and we love familiarity. But inherent to familiarity is a lack of growth. The easiest choice in any day of fishing is going to a familiar bay and making the proverbial milk run to the spots you regularly fish. Make this year the one where you fish three or four new bays. They can be tertiary bays that attach to ones you are already familiar with, or new ones in completely new regions of the coast. Just go fish somewhere new.

Make sure you have a reliable GPS so you do not introduce too much peril into this mini-adventure and can explore a new body of water with some level of confidence. Use the skills you instinctively use as you fish familiar water, but do it in a whole new region. You will be stunned how much it improves your game.

When you are fishing virgin territory, you naturally approach areas with a sense of anticipation and a beginner's spirit. You wade or drift with a heightened sense of attentiveness to your surroundings. Ultimately, you lean out of your comfort zone and learn.

There is a great quote by John Shedd: "A ship in harbor is safe, but that is not what ships are built for." I think that perfectly captures the explorers' spirit that can make all of us better anglers. Every time you stretch to a new bay or even a new shoreline, you are leaving your safe harbor and improving your skills. If you want to guarantee success on your next fishing trip, try a new body of water; and even if you strike out completely, you will undoubtedly leave a better angler. That is true success.

Start a Logbook

It might be an overstatement to say that starting a logbook will make you a better angler today. But, if it is safe to say that starting a retirement account is the origin to making one wealthy, then starting a logbook is undoubtedly the precursor to becoming a better angler. And like investing, the longer you work at it, the more valuable the effort becomes.

Angler logbooks date back to the origins of fishing. I can't imagine the number of triumphs and trials of angling that have been commemorated on everything from cave walls to iPads. Anglers have long chronicled their successes and failures with hopes of discerning patterns in the often-erratic results we all encounter. I started a fishing log as a child and very quickly found that there are some clear and almost glaring macro-patterns to coastal trout and redfish fishing. But there are also a surprising amount of subtle yet very important patterns hidden in the fabric of our days spent fishing. A logbook makes you look at each day critically and forces you to analyze the conditions and results.

The key to a successful fishing log is to make it easy to complete so you actually do it. A blank logbook is worthless, so keep it simple. Utilize your smartphone or tablet to make a basic spreadsheet or Word document template that you can easily complete and store after every trip. Note the key features of the day, where you succeeded, and equally importantly where you failed. Note conditions but, most importantly, the patterns you saw emerge. Also, do not hesitate to add anecdotal

information you picked up from other anglers' results from the day or even reliable fishing reports that may have offered a different outcome than you achieved. In the past, I would even make logbook entries from the results of friends who fished on days that I did not. Their results can provide a crucial clue to stitching together a seasonal pattern. Also, consider overlaying tide, moon, and predictive feeding pattern charts. There are a number of services that provide these, and those additional clues can help in the quest for increased expertise.

The biggest failing in a logbook is not starting it, which is quickly followed by not keeping up with it. Like investing, you cannot start until you set up that first account, so start today by crafting a basic template that you know you will actually use after a long day of fishing. If diligently utilized, that alone will guarantee you better results that can start today and last a lifetime.

Tune Up Your Gear

Keeping your fishing gear in tune is one of the easiest and also most overlooked parts of being a better angler. We anglers are the worst about letting hooks get rusty and dull, letting monofilament line become coiled and dated, and watching braid literally turn dusty before we change it. We let our reels get bogged down with grime, and our pliers become motionless with corrosion. It's really not that hard to keep up with, yet we neglect our gear. If you think about it, you have to have highly functional tools to become a master craftsman, and in angling, the pieces of your fishing gear are your tools. Think about a master chef. Is he or she going to go into a major night of kitchen work with dull knives? Fishing is no different.

As minor as it sounds, taking a moment to run a sharpening stone on the primary jigheads in your wading box or your go-to box on your boat can make the difference in a trip. Years ago, while fishing a tournament, one of my tournament partners Leon Napoli regularly sharpened jigheads during our days fishing together. At first, I thought he was just being obsessive, until his point finally sunk in (not a bad pun). In the tournament, we were only targeting to weigh-in three trout per angler per day. That's essentially three bites. If you are looking for three bites, why are you going to let an even mildly blunted jighead keep you from winning the tournament? If you think about it, the same holds true in a normal day of fishing. None of us get to fish enough, so why would we not do everything possible to increase our advantage to actually catch fish? If the bite is fast, you want to make sure and maximize it,

and if its slow, you surely do not want to miss a single tap. By simply sharpening or changing your hooks and changing your line, you will undoubtedly improve your results.

Simple Steps

There are countless ways for all of us to improve our skill in the art of fishing. This simple list captures just a few, but if you take these to action and look for others in your own quest for improvement, you may find that the best way to become a better angler is found in the simplest steps.

9

Myth Busting

Do more things that make you forget your phone.

—Anonymous

KEY POINTS

- You don't need a big bait to catch big fish. Sure, that long held axiom has some truth, but it is not an exclusive. Using a bait that actually gets bites greatly increases your chances of catching a big fish far more than grinding away with a massive bait just for the sake of using a massive bait.

- Topwaters work in all depths of water. Remember that fish often feed in the top of the water column, and the depth below them is not necessarily relevant.

- There are no secret spots. The key is to realize that you likely already have a number of "secret spots" in your current repertoire, and if you study experts, listen to other angler's insights, keep a detailed fishing log, and work hard at practicing your art, you will build your own secret recipe book.

- There are no obsolete baits. If it was a great bait once, it is probably a great one today.

- The early bird does not always catch the proverbial worm. Remember that fish feed in patterns, and those patterns do not always begin at sunrise.

- No boat does not mean no fish. Although shore-bound anglers are inherently limited in ability to move, they can use their lack of mobility to their advantage by focusing acutely on the areas that they can access.

- There is an aged myth that a crowd will scare fish from feeding or chase them from an area. Often, that is not the case. The hard part of fishing in a crowd is making yourself focus on your pattern and not the distraction of your fellow anglers.

Untangling the Fallacy of Common Fishing Myths

Trying to debunk the countless myths in fishing is one of my favorite efforts. I never cease to be amazed by some of the outlandish restraints anglers impose on themselves because they have an almost genetically coded adherence to some myth that drives them to not do one thing or another because it will surely lead to failure or success. Often, it is more than restrictive. As much as I try to avoid these myths, I still find myself caught in the gillnet of patterns that are tied to some aversion or another that when tested often proves to be silly.

There is a term coined by the renowned writer Nassim Nicholas Taleb known as the *ludic fallacy*. It actually sounds much more complex than it is. Grossly paraphrased, it boils down to the basic human drive to oversimplify the complexity of the world, particularly when it comes to causality and patterns. We love to believe that if you do X, it will always result in Y, and doing Z will never lead to A. Taleb's overriding point is that there is no "always," and I believe there is no better forum to prove his point than in the arena of fishing. We want to believe that an incoming tide and light southeast wind will always produce the angling result we want, and then we become disillusioned when that pattern breaks.

As anglers, we cling to well-worn traditions and, at times, blindly follow them to a fault. Indeed, patterns do occur and there are significant parts of this book that address the importance of those patterns. They can be an important part of consistently producing successful results, but there are also myths and misconceptions that can limit our efforts and, most importantly, our results. Breaking fishing myths might not only break you from the crowd; it might put you on a few more fish.

"You Need a Big Bait to Catch a Big Fish"

No more effective myth exists in fishing. It has led to the creation of absurdly large topwaters, horror-movie-quality soft plastics, and a host of bulbous and tentacled bait variations that tempt even the most level-headed angler. Do large fish succumb to large baits? Absolutely. I have tremendous confidence in targeting big trout with the relatively beastly Heddon Super Spook. Undoubtedly, big baits do catch big fish, but for many anglers in many applications, the big-bait-big-fish mantra sadly translates into a big-bait-no-fish reality.

One of the largest catches of seriously monster trout I ever experienced came several decades ago from the now-defunct Baycliff outlet that poured warmed water into the western wall of upper Galveston Bay. I was fishing in the middle of the night in the dead of a particularly icy winter using live shrimp smaller than my pinky finger. (Side note:

Using spider-sized live shrimp was not a brilliant insight on my part; it was simply all the bait camp had.) The myth would have told you that those trophy trout were laying in the warmer temperature water, hungry for a rhino of a mullet or hand-sized shad. Interestingly, there were anglers who were using those types of baits in the area, but these trout wanted the exact opposite. They were feeding on small crustaceans and (remarkably) snail-like creatures and worms that were tight to the bottom. The fish did not feel the need for a large protein load but instead chose less movement and increased small item intake. Remember that big baits can work, but they are not the exclusive key to catching big fish.

"Topwaters Only Work in Shallow Water"

Like all of these myths, there is some truth here. Indeed, topwaters can be very effective in shallow water, but they should not be discounted in deep water—sometimes very deep water. If you don't believe me, throw a large chrome or bone walking bait behind a culling shrimp boat offshore. Some of the most impressive, jarring strikes I have ever seen came from implementing that very elementary tactic. Watching a twenty-plus pound king mackerel come seemingly from Atlantis to

grab a topwater bait as it blows through the surface is simply staggering. It really makes sense when you think about it. Predators orient to where the food source is. If the bait is on the surface, it really doesn't matter what the depth is.

There are numerous deepwater topwater techniques, ranging from throwing chuggers for yellowfin tuna over a blue water canyon to walking stickbaits while drifting bay reefs for speckled trout and redfish. Ultimately, the surface is the surface. It is a supercharged part of the water column that is often packed with nutrients, energy, and light. It is an electric layer of the bay or ocean and is definitely where all the cool kids hang out. I'm not knocking bottom fish but . . . well . . . just look at the name.

It doesn't take long to determine that topwaters don't always produce in deep water, but it is important to remember that they can produce in deep water. I still vividly remember the first day I was driftfishing with customers over a deep Galveston reef and tied on a Rebel Jumpin' Minnow; I immediately unlocked an all-too-obvious technique that I had never utilized. Of course trout will eat a topwater in open water over deep structure, but this somehow had been lost on me for the years prior. I now commonly throw topwaters while driftfishing in all areas of the Galveston Bay complex if I see even the slightest amount of surface bait activity. It really is an incredibly common pattern that is strangely overlooked and remarkably can outproduce traditional deeper water choices like jigs and sinking plugs. I would not make it your only choice for drifting, but I would definitely make it a top-three choice.

"There Are Secret Spots"

This is the unspoken holy grail of anglers—that mystic spot that is tucked away somewhere between the fountain of youth and Neptune's man cave, where the water is always green and there is somehow always a bite. The allure of the "secret spot" has led hordes of anglers to belittle themselves into lurking at boat docks and sheepishly following a proven angler or acclaimed guide to his or her magic fishing destination. The fact is there are no secret spots.

The current traveling range, electronic sophistication, and angling insight of recreational fishermen via the internet has erased virtually any insider advantage regarding a particular spot. Like imagining there is a secret chord on a guitar or a secret ingredient in a recipe, there rarely is a single new trick or secret insight that makes someone superior. It is more commonly the combination of insight, experience, and expertise that makes the musician, chef, or in our case, angler so much better. This fact is comforting in a way. If it was truly about secret spots, there would be only an exclusive few who would have access to the best of the bay, and the reality is that GPSs largely eliminated that. Just make sure that you don't spend all of your valuable fishing time looking for the magic spot like some sunken treasure. The key is to realize that you likely already have a number of "secret spots" in your current repertoire, and if you study experts, listen to other anglers' insights, keep a detailed fishing log, and work hard at practicing your art, you will build your own secret recipe book.

"That Bait Is Obsolete"

Revered outdoor writer and longtime friend Doug Pike once compared my tackle box to some version of a time capsule for dead and dying coastal lures. I have to admit that his rather harsh assessment is actually not too far off. Although there have been some incredible innovations in light-tackle application lures for speckled trout and red drum (which have a modest but growing presence in my selection), there are also some time-tested designs and colors that may not be the rage, but still exist because they work and will always work. I am not convinced that some version of natural selection has evolved speckled trout to the point that they are beyond falling prey to a silver spoon. Although irrelevant in many anglers' tackle boxes and minds, the time-tested, flashy, wobbly, vibrating dance of a spoon still works, as do shrimp-tails, bucktail jigs, the forgotten hootie rig, and a museum worth of now-misfit and vanishing baits. Honestly, if I had to live off of a single bait, it would be an easy pick for me. I am confident that there is no more adaptable and transportable lure than the spoon. From a Caribbean island to a south Texas grass flat, spoons get bites and always will.

In busting this myth, remember that anglers' tastes change a lot quicker than the drives and motivations of fish. If you have confidence in a bait, use it. I truly believe that our own insecurities lead us to think that we are only as good as the baits in our box, when the reality is that you can take a great fisherman and give him or her as dated a plug or spoon as you can dig up, and they will make it work for them. As the saying goes, "It's all about the archer and not the arrows." Obviously, I love that quote.

"The Early Bird Catches the Worm"

If there is such a thing as a classic fishing myth, the almost instinct-like draw of anglers to be on the water at dawn may be it. It literally transcends time and water type. Be it a remote mountain lake or a blue water platform, anglers are seemingly inseparable from the sunrise.

Like previously addressed myths, the most pervasive are often that way because there is some truth in them and sometimes even a significant amount of truth in them. A lot of fish are caught at first light, particularly during times of hot air and warm water temperatures. But we also have to remember that the fish do not cocoon on the nearest tree limb after the sun has broken well above the horizon.

For that matter, we really should not even assume that they always retreat to the deepest channel at all. Shallow flats anglers often curse the dim light and oppressive crowds of first light as amateur hour. They might even wait to launch their trip after the overpowered and unfocused horde has blown over the shallowest of terrain, allowing them to find the midmorning, regrouped schools to track anonymously.

Just like humans, fish feed in cycles. They have patterns that do follow tide, temperature, light period, and countless other nuances, but the most important thing to remember is that patterns change. To be consistent in angling success, one has to be willing to change to match the evolving manmade and natural patterns. There are plenty of times fish feed at first light, but that does not mean there is not a late day bite that might be more explosive.

Next time your schedule does not allow an early morning departure, even if it's in a classically early-bird spot like wadefishing the surf, pick an accommodative tide later in the day and start grinding. You may find a new pattern and bust an age-old myth.

"No Boat, No Fish"

As one who does not currently own a boat and largely fishes the upper Texas coast, I understand the sting of the "no boat equals no fish" mantra. At times, it is very hard to argue. Boatless anglers are often left with few entry points and little mobility, but the key is to use the often-limited angling access to your full advantage. In an era when a bay boat with a two hundred–horsepower motor can be considered sluggish, the attraction of high-speed spot changes and the overall abdication of careful patrolling for fish signs have taken control of the fishing pattern of a majority of anglers.

Through my years of fishing in and around the frustratingly few walk-in access points of both Galveston's East and West Bays, I have always felt that less choices make fishing a true test of both focus and patience. If you cannot change spots, it takes a lot of temptation out of the equation. In picking your spot, you want to maximize your odds by understanding the macro seasonal patterns, tide height and velocity, and wind direction for the small selection of available spots. Make your best call, and use focus to your advantage. You will likely not be able to change your location dramatically once you arrive, so regardless if you are shore fishing or wadefishing, thoroughly fish your spot.

If your legs are your sole transportation, use your ability to fish longer hours and concentrate on the habitat you have available to maximize your catch. Assess the area that you have to fish not unlike you might approach a small farm pond. Note anything that feeds the area habitat, like a bayou inlet or deep channel. Consider the seasonal pattern and the general trend for fish to be on either a hard or softer bottom, and most importantly, use your eyes to inventory any baitfish activity. Take nothing for granted, because in reality, it might be all you have.

Finally, let time work for you. If your schedule allows and the conditions look somewhat accommodative, grind it out. If the choice is struggling in a marginally productive cove or shoreline or watching a ballgame on TV at home, the choice is easy. I have walked into many strikeout sessions, but I can clearly remember some of my most rewarding coming from walking into truly world-class fishing. If you are adaptable and focused, you never have to forgo fishing just because you don't have a boat.

Additionally, the advent of kayaks and stand-up paddleboards has changed the access game entirely. Now an angler can make a much smaller investment than a full boat, motor, and trailer, and get a kayak or paddleboard that can open up vast shorelines and backwater areas. Having a boat is definitely an advantage, but walking or paddling in can often be just as rewarding.

"You Can't Catch Fish If Its Crowded"

I understand the unattractive parts of fishing in a crowd. For my regular fishing compadres, my propensity to avoid crowds could even appear masochistic. I have been known to leave fish simply because of the boat traffic. Please don't think me to be a snob or one of those outrageously ridiculous folks who scream at any boat that comes within eyesight of them. I am definitely not that, but I find that the bigger the crowd, the more difficult it is to enjoy myself.

There are times, though, when the crowds are simply on the fish, and maybe the only active schools of fish in the entire bay. There is an aged myth that a crowd will scare fish from feeding or chase them from an area. The spoiler to this illusion is the amount of different schools of fish in the area. If there are enough fish, they can accommodate a staggering number of boats and anglers.

Anyone who fished Galveston's East Bay in the early summer of 2015 and 2016 knows that when freshwater concentrates large and multiple schools of speckled trout in small portions of a bay, you can catch fish in almost any sized crowd.

By no means am I suggesting using the clueless horde as a gauge of fish locations, but if you truly want to catch fish and the fish are indeed concentrated in a small area for an extended time, there may not be a choice. In these situations, the key to maintaining your sanity and maximizing your catch is to focus on your fishing and not everything going on around you. Watching the variety of boats or waders catching or for that matter not catching fish can completely destroy your concentration. Focus on the area and what you have traditionally done to catch fish. Use other anglers to refine your strategy, but never use them to define it. If you are focusing on the folks around you, you are definitely not focusing on patterning your quarry. Crowds can be limiting, but they never mark an end to your fishing options.

Break Your Own Myths

There are some treasured myths and wonderful folklore embedded in coastal angling. Most of it is well intended and anchored in some truth. But ultimately, every angler needs to create his and her own standards for fishing. Take a moment and think through any myths that are self-imposed or that you have picked up through your travels and ground truth them. If you start to dig through your own thought processes, you might be surprised at how many sub- and semiconscious decisions are made based on a general feeling that is attached to an outdated or outright false belief. Bust your own set of myths, and you will undoubtedly become a better angler.

10

The Power of Conservation

The charm of fishing is that it is the pursuit of what is elusive but attainable, a perpetual series of occasions for hope.

–John Buchan

KEY POINT

- Anglers can be the best advocates for our shared coastal resources. It is critically important that we all get involved in conservation.

A NUMBER OF years ago, in preparing for a presentation at a philanthropy round table, I stumbled on the above quote by Scottish philosopher John Buchan. I have used the quote many, many times since in writings and in talks with all types of groups, and it never seems to lose its impact and clarifying power as to the allure of fishing.

As any angler can attest, Buchan managed to almost perfectly capture the addictive draw of fishing, but more importantly, he (likely unintentionally) identified the pathway to the powerful conservation tradition found in recreational angling. If you examine the history of marine conservation victories in the past half century, you will quickly find that the majority of them have been launched, driven, and even funded by recreational anglers. What Buchan may not have intended to capture in his amazing quote is that the ephemeral occasion for hope that emerges with every cast in angling also drives an enduring passion. And that passion to catch a fish quickly turns into a passion to make a difference in the future of the coastal resources we value. It fuels your next cast but also may fuel a willingness to join marine resource advocacy groups, participate in habitat restoration projects, or even just exercise a little voluntary restraint and regularly release fish. It is a truly amazing phenomenon.

A great example is the groundswell of support that drove the Texas Parks and Wildlife Commission to take visionary action in Texas coastal waters a number of years ago to reduce the speckled trout limit from ten fish to five along the majority of the coast. The science was not 100 percent conclusive that there was a significant problem with the stock, but many recreational anglers sensed a danger to the stock in the harvest levels and wanted to be proactive. If you really think about it, that type of vision is rare and can only come from a selfless desire to protect and enhance the resources that we all enjoy. That is truly powerful.

So why would some resource-focused organizations and federal government agencies ever seek to arbitrarily limit or even exclude recreational anglers when they are key drivers for conservation and are a growing source of economic output for the nation? It is difficult to figure out the exact motivation, but it is an unfortunate reality that has existed for decades and might even be accelerating.

Remember that recreational anglers are often a catalyst for positive regulation and have a long history of embracing bag, size, and even seasonal limits when they make sound conservation sense. A number of years ago, I wrote a somewhat-glib opinion column about the accelerating trend toward excluding recreational anglers from ocean resources and decided to readdress the topic in this book, with an eye toward the management challenges we currently face. Although opinions of this nature are commonly categorized as alarmist, they really are grounded in a looming federal management trend that is becoming all too prevalent. If you believe that great conservation comes from passion, then it is impossible to argue for practices that diminish well-managed participation by recreational anglers. Our ocean access is not necessarily disappearing overnight, but if we fall asleep, we will surely wake up to a much smaller ocean.

A Disappearing Ocean?

Does the ocean make a sound if there is no one there to hear it? I know that reads like a silly dip into existentialism, but it begs a relevant question of anglers. Are we gradually losing recreational fishing access to our nation's waters and particularly federal waters? It's a simple question. And if the direction of the National Marine Fisheries Service and a number of other federal management agencies is any indicator, I fear the answer becomes obvious.

There are a growing number of examples of this alarming trend. In 2015, the US National Park Service disappointed anglers with a misguided closure of parts of the Biscayne National Park to recreational anglers, the National Marine Fisheries Service (NMFS) continues its drive of the past decade to privatize key reef fish species in the Gulf of Mexico for commercial harvesters, and the threat of large ocean access closure always looms with ongoing discussions of massive webs of exclusionary marine protected areas. It seems nonsensical but persists even in the face of an ocean of evidence indicating that more recreational anglers create more conservation.

Arguably, the most fundamental need of recreational angling is access. If you are prohibited from fishing, all of the complications of tide, wind, feeding patterns, difficult bites, and every other nuance in successful angling that you have been reading about in this book become irrelevant. If you can't go fishing, it really doesn't matter if the fish are not biting or even there. The "occasion for hope" is gone. As the conservation visionary Walter Fondren III once pointed out to me, if the recreational anglers are not present to steward the resource, it surely falls prey to commercial overharvest or rout exclusion. Undoubtedly, if recreational anglers had not cared about catching red drum along the Texas coast, that stock would have been permanently decimated if not eliminated by commercial overharvest in the 1970s.

The most popular recreational fishery in the United States is largemouth bass. Ask yourself why that is. Is it their sprinting runs across air-clear grass flats? Their nonstop, Olympic-quality acrobatics? Michelin-star quality table fare? I would argue that although they are an incredibly desirable sport fish to pursue and a lot of fun to catch, their unique and ubiquitous appeal is largely driven by the fact that an eager angler of any age is rarely more than a short drive, bike ride, or even walk from a pond, lake, reservoir, or river that houses one of these fine fish. It is access that helps them be the target of countless angler trips a year.

The lovable finfish species of our oceans and bays will always have a distinct disadvantage in luring prospective suitors. By proximity, saltwater is quite a bit more difficult and often more expensive to access. Although favorable improvements in so many forms of transportation have aided the ease of accessing coastal destinations, it is almost always going to be easier for a landlocked angler to access a largemouth over a saltwater species.

So why would a national parks service or federal fisheries management agency seek to limit recreational angling in a marine-centered national park or in US federal waters? Why would there be near-constant rumblings of potential massive marine no-fishing zones being created via the Antiquities Act at the end of virtually every presidential term in the past two decades? I apparently missed when it was determined that recreational angling was such an imminent and imposing threat to the future of our nation's fisheries and the integrity of federal parks to the point that it needed to be banned. Statistically, recreational anglers have historically taken a mere 2 percent of the nation's harvest of marine finfish, as opposed to the 98 percent harvested by commercial fishermen. Shockingly, recreational anglers string up literally billions of dollars in economic output annually, while commercial fishermen bring in a fraction of that dollar amount while harvesting more than 90 percent of the annual capture of marine species. Yet the federal fisheries management system is regularly trying to promote and perpetuate commercial fisheries by creating privatized harvest rights and subsidies.

So, are our shared oceans disappearing? In many ways, they are not. But if access is denied or even grows measurably more restrictive, the answer is a resounding and haunting "yes."

I am often asked what an angler can do to make a difference, and the answer is simple: get involved in marine conservation. It really is not that hard because there are so many entry points into this important effort. It can be as simple as joining a marine resource advocacy group. I have an obvious bias for the Coastal Conservation Association (CCA), but there are a lot of great groups on the state and federal level that you can join. Honestly, you should likely look into all of them and join the one or ones that fit your interests.

The next step is to start getting involved. This can be as basic as reaching out to your state and federal elected leaders and letting them know that you are a recreational angler and an important part of the

economy. The great thing about marine resource conservation is that you can get as involved as much as you would like. I know folks who work just as hard or, dare I write, even harder in their volunteer service as they do in their full-time job. It can become an overwhelmingly addictive passion when you realize the difference one concerned angler can make. I strongly suggest that if you are not already active, start today. It may not make you a better angler, but it will surely make the resources you so dearly love stronger and healthier.

11

Never Stop Learning

Never lose your beginner's spirit.
—Thirteenth-century Japanese proverb

KEY POINTS

- Look to the bass angling world to learn the next new technique, bait, or technology. Bass anglers have led to as much innovation in saltwater recreational angling as any other influence.

- Look at other fisheries (both abroad and in your backyard) to find new applications for proven techniques. Fish are fish, and something that makes a northern pike bite might entice a speckled trout as well.

- Think about rutted trails through a forest. Maybe they are paths because they avoid some pitfall, but likely they are simply a route that someone pioneered and everyone else blindly followed. With this in mind, try to fish a new spot every fishing trip.

- Make sure you master the spots you frequent. Avoid the rush to the hot spot, and explore every dimension of the spot to fully understand it.

- Remember that no pattern is permanent nor without exceptions, and no technique is foolish. Keep your beginner's spirit, and you will never stop improving.

THINK ABOUT how excited you were when you first started fishing. If you were like me, thoughts and dreams of fishing flooded your head as a child to the point of detention-invoking distraction. I would etch images of every species I ever pursued or wanted to pursue, created wildly inaccurate but vividly detailed fishing maps of the places my dad and I fished, and all the while, I generally obsessed about all things fishing. I was willing to fish anywhere anytime, even if pesky obligations like school, work, eating, and all of the trappings of conventional life threatened to encumber me. I never cared about the direction or velocity of the wind or the drizzling rain or even a potential crowd on the water. I simply went fishing with complete enthusiasm anytime I had a chance. That beginner's spirit is the proverbial x factor in all parts of life that separates great from good. There are lots of people who want to be better anglers, but some make it a lifestyle. And when I write "lifestyle," I don't necessarily mean they are full-time fishing guides or professional anglers; they just never lose the beginner's spirit and enthusiasm.

They relish the angling experience, hunger to improve, and honestly know that they will continue to get better. It's that same spirit that leads to innovation and excellence in any space, and there is good reason to remember and reignite that drive in your pursuit of fishing. I have listed a few reminders that I use to keep my angling perspective fresh and that push me out of my comfort zone and into new patterns. I have lightly touched some of these themes throughout this book, but I think it is important to highlight these important factors to help keep a fresh perspective on angling. Try these, and make sure you also take a moment to mentally or physically note a few of your own key drivers.

Keep Your Eye on Bass Fishermen

Bass anglers do not get enough credit for their transformative impact on the inshore marine angling space. In my years of fishing, I have seen more innovation in baits and techniques come from bass anglers than from any other space. For speckled trout and redfish anglers, we owe them a priceless debt of gratitude for some of the most useful and exciting parts of our modern angling techniques. Think about it. Bass fishermen were regularly using topwater baits when most trout fishermen of that time thought a rattling cork over a live shrimp was innovative. They used jerkworms in dozens of applications before saltwater anglers ever thought to stick a Slug-O on a jighead and were born into the era of Bass Assassins. Think about it. They are called *Bass Assassins*. The list goes on: crankbaits, trolling motors, floater-divers, scented baits and sprays, and spinnerbaits. You get the point. Bass anglers and their associated innovations in tackle and techniques have always led the saltwater space.

So why do we not look to that arena regularly for fresh ideas? I was recently at the Bassmaster Classic and watched some portions of the weigh-in. As various teams hit new heights in their weights, they were often queried what bait they were using. I was struck that in close to an hour of listening to various bass pros, I recognized only two baits. It was a great reminder that I am not paying enough attention to their vision and innovation.

It would be foolish to blindly start throwing the newest hot bass lure, but it is reasonable to make sure you wander over to the freshwater hard and soft bait aisles during your next tackle run. Scan a catalog or two and maybe . . . just maybe . . . buy a bass fishing magazine. You can ask them to put it in one of the brown paper bags they put the porn in, or better yet, get a tablet version in the privacy of your home. (No one will ever know.) Check out what is working and, more importantly, why and how the bass pros are doing it. Think about the crossover potential and how it could improve some of your current approaches. Finally, take a bass technique and use it to pioneer an entirely new pattern—maybe flipping a jig along a steep bank or running a spinnerbait or swimming bait along some boat docks or pier pilings. If history is an indicator, bass fishermen are likely using our next great bait right now. We just don't know it yet.

Look at Other Fisheries

I vividly remember reading the legendary Atlantic longliner Linda Greenlaw's book *Hungry Ocean*, and her description about the attention she and her colleagues spent tracking sometimes-subtle ocean temperature changes, looking for baitfish, and sighting open-ocean birds to help them locate swordfish. I was incredulous. Why would these folks ever need to look for fish signs? They use ridiculously destructive gear composed of thousands of hooks spread over miles of ocean. But it finally occurred to me that fish are fish and patterns can matter a lot, even when you use thousands of hooks. There are patterns that are traditional for any bay or bay complex, but don't be afraid to look for patterns from other bays, coasts, or even countries to import something new to your portfolio of ideas.

It has been interesting through the past decades to watch various trout and redfish techniques spread along the Texas coast. As anglers became more mobile due to larger outboards, greater fuel capacity, and a relentless willingness to trailer boats long distances, patterns that were only seen in certain discreet areas began to work in new regions. This was not due to some tectonic shift in feeding patterns of fish but rather a change in angler approach. I remember fishing with colleagues who guided in south Texas and regularly used a thin clicker cork (referred to as a Mansfield Mauler back then), and I thought that might help me with customers who struggled to keep a jig out of shell in super-shallow water in some of the tertiary lakes off of Galveston's West Bay. I grabbed a few clicker corks and quickly learned that it not only helped an occasional customer keep their bait out of oyster shells; it actually started to produce more fish on certain occasions. Not unlike my previous references to the largemouth bass angling world, there are countless examples of other baits and techniques that have seeped from bay to bay and state to state, and have added valuable depth to anglers' skills. It really just takes keeping your eyes and mind open to new ideas.

As you read angling publications that touch multiple bays and, even better, multiple regions with diverse fisheries, think about how some of the techniques you see could fit into your current patterns. Remember that a bait that seduces a snook will likely fool a trout and a spoon that deceives a pike might very well entice a redfish.

It's exciting to think about the areas that were once deemed dead water or unwadeable that are now hot-spot destinations, or baits that were thought to be regional that now fill a key spot in every angler's box. It reminds us all that there is still so much untapped potential to improve our angling. We just have to keep looking.

Don't Fish the Same Spot Twice. . . .

Maybe the only thing more patterned than fish are the fishermen who pursue them. We are the worst about getting into ruts in fishing. I think some of that is driven by convenience, but probably the strongest driver is our uncanny ability to cling to past victories. We often fish memories rather than patterns. We pursue and repursue that legendary trip when everything made sense and every move was correct. It's hard not to, but it is one of our greatest traps.

Think about rutted trails through a forest. Maybe they are paths because they avoid some pitfall, but likely they are simply a route that someone pioneered and everyone else blindly followed. With this in mind, try to fish a new spot every fishing trip. That might be difficult with limited hours in any trip or a limited ability to get to new spots due to lack of access, but think about how you can fish a new spot even if it is just slightly off one of your rutted trails. This will not only open new doors for new fishing spots but will also make you refresh your beginner's spirit. It is hard not to get excited when you are trying a new area if you have the right attitude toward it.

. . . Then Fish It a Hundred Times

Now, I will take the opposite side of the advice of the previous paragraph and recommend that you thoroughly learn the spots that you regularly fish. To this day, I go to spots that I have fished both successfully and unsuccessfully, and suddenly find a fresh nuance that adds significantly to the value of the spot. A new stretch of broken shell or a subtle change in bay bottom texture can give you a new perspective on how to better leverage a spot or possibly find some aspect that may make it viable in seasons, winds, or salinity that you previously would consider out-of-bounds. Make sure you know the areas that you fish, and try to avoid missing the whole picture in your effort to rush to the proverbial sweet spot. You may find that you were missing a far bigger pattern.

Fish the Unfishable

There are no bad spots or nonsensical patterns if you really think about it. Odds are that virtually every spot in a bay has some fish on it at some point. I know that is a bit absurd, but think of the cliché image of the broken watch that is accurate twice a day. Clearly, there are massive stretches of bays that are at best transient highways for passing fish and see little or no feeding activity. But there are also spots that are thought to be dead water that likely teem with fish, if only for a tide or two, and patterns that appear nonsensical but are filled with opportunity at certain periods.

In full confession, I can indict myself on ignoring some potential opportunities for my entire angling history. I remember numerous conversations in the past with fellow anglers and guides about the series of reefs and guts on the western face of the Galveston causeway, stretching from the area southwest of the Tiki Channel across the bay to South Deer Island. You can look on any map or low-tide satellite image and see ridges of exposed oyster reef, vivid guts, tidal washouts, and every other textbook "fish here" sign you would care to fantasize about. I talked about the unlocked potential and can even recall a couple of half-hearted attempts when fishing with the late (and very great) Pete Tanner in the early 1990s. We made a few weak attempts to fish some reef points and drift some guts, only to hurry to the spot we really wanted to go to in West Bay or at the Causeway pilings. I am confident someone or maybe many anglers have since unlocked that pattern, but it stands as a classic example of how easy it is to not explore. I would speculate that everyone reading this has a spot or two that they have wanted to explore, but the draw of perennial favorites and the squeeze of not enough days on the water make us walk the same trail, regardless of the rut.

At the advent of the Troutmasters Tournament series, there was a fascinating collection of great trout anglers along the Texas coast who were regularly pushed out of their comfort zone by the tournament organizers, who moved the tournament destination along the entire coast. Exceptionally gifted fishermen found themselves in completely foreign water, and not unlike the tournament bass anglers, they relied on their general sense, experience, a little prefishing, and the ability to grind out a spot. Having participated in a handful of these tournaments, I found myself in a number of truly foreign bodies of water, which was an eye-opening experience. But what I found far more revealing was watching foreign anglers in my regular spots. There is no better learning experience than watching unacquainted anglers fish an area you know well. They may approach it differently (that is code for "wrongly") or fish it under conditions I would feel make no sense. The funny part about that experience was when their seemingly absurd pattern or approach turned out right and my hard-earned knowledge of the area was wrong.

I remember a tournament when there had been a phenomenal bite for big trout on the north shoreline of Galveston's East Bay during prefishing, but a massive front dramatically dropped the tide and (in my mind) made the shoreline untenable. A number of anglers who were not regulars to that bay were left with few alternatives and decided to grind it out, wading way out on the shoreline over a seemingly barren mud flat. You probably can guess the conclusion of the story. They won. I didn't. At the weigh-in, in disbelief, I saw these solid catches come from what I would have deemed a fool's journey. It turns out that this pattern works from time to time. It is not even close to a sure bet, but I have used those anglers' insights to this day to catch fish on a pattern I once thought silly. It is a true learning experience when you get one of your own unspoken personal myths busted.

The lesson here becomes redundant. Remember that no pattern is permanent nor without exceptions, and no technique is foolish. Keep your beginner's spirit, and you will never stop improving.

12

Bringing It All Together

Art (noun)—The expression or application of human creative skill and imagination.

WHEN PURSUED by a person with the correct attitude and perspective, fishing is undoubtedly as much an art as painting, cooking, dance, martial arts, or any other lasting human expression of craftsmanship or skill. Somewhere along the way, through the decades or even centuries, the understanding of fishing as art got confused in the minds of many. I get it. Those who are outside of our beloved pursuit might see it as a random walk to a body of water, followed by the hapless, unfocused thrashing of fishing gear. That could not be more wrong, but nonetheless, it is the perspective of many who will likely largely remain unchangeable and will either disregard or outright dislike angling. To me, the unfortunate part of the mind-set that angling is a purely chance-driven game is that it diminishes those who have elevated the pursuit to a zen-like level and also likely inhibits others from having the proper perspective to get there. If you think of long-distance running, rock climbing, writing, or anything for that matter as a pedestrian pursuit, then you will never reach excellence and clearly never master the essence of any of them. Fishing is no different. The first step is to acknowledge that there is a lot more to it than sharp hooks and chance encounters. Once you begin to work at it like an art, you really start to elevate your performance and subsequently your results.

There is a great expression that "your life will go in the direction of your thoughts." Fishing is no exception. If you think of it as a masterable pursuit with tangible steps for improvement, you have set the framework for a plan to become excellent. Combine a little drive and the incredible power of experience, and you are there.

Remember that the best in any human effort don't get there by accident. We all want to think excellence is the luck of the draw or some gift of genetics. There is always a seductively easy and often incorrect answer for why someone achieves greatness. In our hearts, we all know excellence is largely earned. It doesn't come in the form of a lottery ticket and has more value than any hard asset because it truly is priceless. It defines success.

A classic example is seen in professional athletics. It is an excuse to say that an individual is only a professional athlete because of their genetic code. Honestly, in the majority of cases, that is a disservice to the discipline, time, dedication, focus, and passion of that athlete. There are a lot of people born with professional athlete bodies who never get close. The different ones are just that—they are different. As grandiose

as this sounds, it is true in the art of fishing as well. You don't have to fish around truly great anglers long to see it in them. It is not just the consistency or ability to seemingly always pull a fish out of their hat. More often than not, it is the apparent ease in which they do it. It is almost effortless—sometimes maddeningly so—but we have to always remember that excellence is earned by time, effort, and attention, and that it can be achieved no matter where you start on the pathway to expertise.

If you want to be the guy or gal who goes out and idly fishes without care of catching anything, then you probably would not be reading this book, and you surely would not have gotten to this closing chapter. My writing style is far too preachy to tolerate if you are not on a much-broader personal journey to get better at your art. There are plenty of anglers who simply want to go and enjoy the day, and the prospect of actually catching fish is a remote extra. There is absolutely nothing wrong with that—we need more people enjoying the resource in as many positive ways as possible. But most folks who go fishing want to catch a fish, and if they can catch a bunch of them, all the better.

The fact that you have read this book likely means that you are or surely will be an accomplished angler. That is not due to any of the insights or ideas of this book, but rather that you have the intention to get better. If you keep that intention burning, that is the engine for change and ultimately for success.

As I have mentioned throughout this publication, it is pivotal to never stop learning and listening. There are so many amazing anglers in this world that there is an almost unlimited supply of great information in books, podcasts, lectures, articles, blogs, and every other means of communication. The two key pieces of the puzzle that no one can give you are the drive to improve your skills and the experience you will gain with every trip. These intangibles are what make anglers great, so the next step for all of us to take is to make sure we actually go fishing.

Don't Forget to Fish

I felt it important to end this book with an adaption of a piece I wrote for *Tide* magazine, titled "Don't Forget to Fish." Late winter and early spring are traditionally times in Texas (among many areas) when trade shows and cable fishing shows occupy anglers' time more than actual fishing. Colder temperatures, rain, fog, and the myriad of normal weather patterns for those seasons create a tremendous inhibition among many anglers and can set the pace for a year of excuses for not going, rather than pressing through the circumstances to go fishing and improve our skills. After the original version of the article was published, I received an outpouring of comments from readers. I assure you this was not due to some prowess of crafting the written word. It was simply because we all forget to fish. Anglers spend so much time on so many aspects of their beloved pursuit of angling, but spend shockingly little time pursuing it. I truly think sometimes we forget to actually go fishing. Like some fine bottle of wine or great craft beer that withers in a storage rack, we savor the thought of it and forget to open it until it has turned to vinegar or stale barley water.

I get it. Most of us, myself included, live relatively or even extremely far from the saltwater we dream to fish. Families, jobs, personal commitments, and a host of other distractions and interests keep us from going fishing, to the point that our love of fishing becomes an almost virtual experience. We walk the aisles at tackle shops, travel to tackle

and boat shows, and peruse the internet looking for fishing reports and photos of those who actually go fishing. It's easy to lose touch with how much time we dedicate to all aspects of fishing *other than* actually fishing.

No one ever spent their waning moments on the proverbial death bed and thought, "If I had only spent more time reading fishing reports on the internet," or "Oh, to be back picking through the value bin of soft plastics at the tackle store." If we added up all the hours, days, and maybe even weeks spent dreaming and not doing, it would make our inner-angler start screaming.

Please know that I wrote this about myself as much as anglers in general. I have commonly found myself with a day off and an invite to go fishing, and unbelievably, I weighed the fact that it was going to be a bit rainy or windy and travel had me behind on emails . . . please. Why would I ever pass up a day to possibly get a bite and to definitely improve my skills by trying? So I could get caught up on emails?

Also, remember that just because you are a diehard coastal angler does not mean you can't throw a jerk worm to an eager largemouth bass at the local community pond or target a tenacious bluegill at a golf course water trap. Everyday fishing makes you a better angler. Additionally, I find that the more I fish, the more connected I am to the value of the resource. The more I value the resource, the harder I work and volunteer to ensure its strength and health.

Take your child fishing. Take your family fishing. Take your parents fishing, or even just take yourself fishing. The most important thing is to make sure you actually go fishing.

Index

Other Books in the Harte Research Institute for Gulf of Mexico Studies Series

Coral Reefs of the Southern Gulf of Mexico
Edited by John W. Tunnell, Ernesto A. Chávez, and Kim Withers

Arrecifes Coralinos del sur del Golfo de México
Edited by John W. Tunnell, Ernesto A. Chávez, and Kim Withers

The Gulf of Mexico Origin, Waters, and Biota:
Volume I, Biodiversity
Edited by Darryl L. Felder and David K. Camp

The Gulf of Mexico Origin, Waters, and Biota:
Volume 2, Ocean and Coastal Economy
Edited by James C. Cato

The Gulf of Mexico Origin, Waters, and Biota:
Volume 3, Geology
Edited by Noreen A. Buster and Charles W. Holmes

The Gulf of Mexico Origin, Waters, and Biota:
Volume 4, Ecosystem-Based Management
Edited by John W. Day and Alejandro Yáñez-Arancibia

The Gulf of Mexico Origin, Waters, and Biota:
Volume 5, Chemical Oceanography
Edited by Thomas S. Bianchi

Encyclopedia of Texas Seashells: Identification, Ecology,
Distribution, and History
John W. Tunnell, Jean Andrews, Noe C. Barrera,
and Fabio Moretzsohn

Sea-Level Change in the Gulf of Mexico
Richard A. Davis

Marine Plants of the Texas Coast
Roy L. Lehman

Beaches of the Gulf Coast
Richard A. Davis

Texas Seashells: A Field Guide
John W. Tunnell, Noe C. Barrera, and Fabio Moretzsohn

Benthic Foraminifera of the Gulf of Mexico:
Distribution, Ecology, Paleoecology
C. Wylie Poag

The American Sea: A Natural History of the Gulf of Mexico
Rezneat Milton Darnell

Birdlife of the Gulf of Mexico
Joanna Burger

Sea Change: A Message of the Oceans
Sylvia Earle